CONTEMPORARY'S

COMMUNICATION SKILLS THAT WORK

A Functional Approach for Life and Work

BOOK ONE

WENDY STEIN

Project Editor
Julie Landau

Consultant
Jorie W. Philippi
Performance Plus Learning
Consultants

CB
CONTEMPORARY
BOOKS
CHICAGO

Photo credits: p. 1—© Dan McCoy/ Rainbow; pp. 3, 9a, 9b—© AP/ Wide World Photos; p. 6a—© Alexander Lowry/ Photo Researchers, Inc.; p. 6b—© Renee Lynn/ Photo Researchers, Inc.; p. 17—© Bill Stanton/ Rainbow; p. 25—© Richard Hutchings/ Info Edit; p. 33—© Rapho/ Photo Researchers, Inc.; p. 41—© Rhoda Sidney/ Photo Edit; pp. 65, 75—© Research Plus; p. 73—© M. Richards/ Photo Edit; p. 91—© Ulrike Welsch/ Photo Researchers, Inc.; p. 107—© Christopher Morrow/ Photo Researchers, Inc.

Library of Congress Cataloging-in-Publication Data

Communication skills that work.
    Contents : bk. 1. A functional approach for life and work / Wendy Stein—bk. 2. A functional approach for life and work / Elizabeth Romanek.
    1. Communication.   I. Stein, Wendy.
P90.S799   1991   302.2   91-11340
ISBN 0-8092-4122-6
ISBN 0-8092-4121-8

Published by Contemporary Books, Inc.
180 North Michigan Avenue, Chicago, Illinois 60601
Manufactured in the United States of America
International Standard Book Number: 0-8092-4122-6

Published simultaneously in Canada by
Fitzhenry & Whiteside
195 Allstate Parkway
Valleywood Business Park
Markham, Ontario L3R 4T8
Canada

Editorial Director
Caren Van Slyke

Editorial
Craig Bolt
Mark Boone
Elizabeth Romanek
Janice Bryant
Holly Graskewitz
Laura Larson
Robin O'Connor

Editorial Assistant
Erica Pochis

Editorial Production Manager
Norma Fioretti

Cover photograph © C. C. Cain

Production Editor
Jean Farley Brown

Cover Design
Georgene Sainati

Illustrator
Graziano, Krafft & Zale, Inc.

Art & Production
Carolyn Hopp
Rosemary Morrissey-Herzberg
Lois Stein

Typography
Ellen Yukel

Photo Research
Research Plus

Contents

TO THE STUDENT....................................iv

UNIT ONE: SPEAKING AND LISTENING 1
Lesson 1: The Communication Process 3
Lesson 2: Communication Strategies 9
Lesson 3: Listening to Instructions 17
Lesson 4: Giving Directions...........................25
Lesson 5: Using the Telephone 33
Lesson 6: Getting Information 41
Lesson 7: Making and Responding to Requests 49
Lesson 8: Problem Solving 57
Lesson 9: Interviews and Job Reviews.................65

UNIT TWO: WRITING...............................73
Lesson 10: Labels and Lists...........................75
Lesson 11: Filling Out Forms 83
Lesson 12: Filling Out Charts.......................91
Lesson 13: Writing Signs and Notes 99

REVIEW 107

ANSWER KEY 113

To the Student

Welcome to *Communication Skills That Work, Book One*. This book is designed to help you learn strategies for communicating more effectively in everyday life and at work. In each lesson, you will see how a listening, speaking, or writing skill is used in everyday life. Then you will learn to apply that skill on the job. Throughout the book, you will have many chances to practice communication skills and to relate them to your own life.

Each chapter contains

- an opening story that puts communication skills in a real-life context
- instruction on effective communication skills
- activities that help you practice those skills
- *Applying Your Skills*, an activity that helps you use the skills in everyday life
- *Problem Solver*, an exercise in which you examine a typical on-the-job problem and arrive at solutions

Some of the activities in this book require you to work with a partner or in a group. However, you can complete most of the activities by yourself. Even if you are not in a class, you might be able to find another person who will do some of the partner activities with you.

The book contains a number of *Practice* exercises. There is an answer key in the back of the book. However, there are no "right" answers for many of the exercises. As you think about and discuss the exercises, you will probably come up with several answers. Always think of good reasons to support your answer.

We hope that you enjoy this book!

Speaking and Listening

In what ways do football players and coaches communicate with each other?

Imagine that you are a football player. You probably listen carefully to your coach's instructions. You ask questions to make sure you understand what you are supposed to do. On the field, you give signals to the other players. You are communicating all the time.

At work and in everyday life, clear communication is vital. In Lesson 1 of this book, you will learn about the features of clear communication and assess your own communication needs. Lesson 2 provides you with specific strategies for listening and speaking more effectively. You will learn to concentrate to better understand what another person is saying. You will also experiment with different speaking and listening techniques.

In Lessons 3 through 9, you will become more aware of what you need to do to communicate more clearly in different everyday and workplace situations. For instance, imagine that a stranger approaches you on the street and asks for directions to a nearby subway stop. Your directions must be simple and precise. Similarly, when you instruct a coworker, you need to be clear and concise. Other lessons will cover situations such as community and work-related meetings, personal and business phone calls, and performance evaluations. You will also learn strategies for effective problem-solving.

The Communication Process

May I Take Your Order?

Mr. Lee was reading the menu at Marlene's Restaurant. Jenna, one of the waitresses, came over to his table.

"Hi," she smiled. "Are you ready to order?"

"Yes, I'll have the cheeseburger deluxe, medium rare."

"OK," Jenna said, and began writing on her order pad.

"Does that come with lettuce and tomato?" Mr. Lee asked.

Jenna nodded her head.

"Well, I want the lettuce and tomato on the side, please," he explained.

"Would you like french fries or potato chips?" Jenna asked.

"French fries, please."

"What kind of cheese would you like?" she asked.

"American."

"Now, let me see if I have your order right. You want the cheeseburger deluxe, with American cheese, cooked medium rare. And you want that with french fries and with lettuce and tomato on the side."

"Right." Mr. Lee nodded his head.

This waitress at a '50s-style restaurant needs to have excellent communication skills.

"How about something to drink?" asked Jenna.

"I'll have a Coke," replied Mr. Lee.

"Thank you," Jenna said, taking Mr. Lee's menu. "Your order will be up shortly."

Jenna walked back to the kitchen. She wrote the order neatly on a small piece of paper so the cook could read it. Then, she placed the piece of paper on the counter and shouted, "Ordering!"

Talk About It

- In what ways does Jenna communicate at her job?
- Why are communication skills important for Jenna to do her job well?
- In what ways do you communicate with other people?

What Is Communication?

The objects below are ways to communicate a message.

► Which of these have you used?

_____

► What other means can you think of to communicate a message?

_____

Communication is a part of everyday life. Communication also plays an important role in your relationships with people, family, friends, coworkers, and so on. When you communicate with someone, you give or receive a message—information, ideas, or feelings.

The diagram at the right shows the three major parts of the communication process: the **sender** passes along a **message** to the **receiver**.

The Communication Process

(Sender)

Speaker

Message

(Receiver)

Listener

Communication takes place only if the receiver understands the sender's message. Communication requires the participation of both the sender and the receiver.

▼ Practice

Record some messages you received this week on a chart like the one below. Use a separate sheet of paper.

Summary of Message	Way of Receiving Message	Who Sent Message?
Deena's school closed because of snowstorm	radio	news reporter
Reminder about doctor's appointment tomorrow	phone call	secretary
Request to work overtime next week	note	boss

Communicating Clearly

▶ Read each of the cartoons. Which of them is an example of good communication? Which of them is an example of poor communication?

Cartoon A

Cartoon B

Did you notice that Cartoon A is an example of successful communication? Why? The store clerk (receiver) understands the customer's (sender's) message. How did the store clerk take responsibility for receiving the message? She listened carefully. Then she restated the customer's information in his own words as she wrote it down.

Did you notice that communication did not occur in Cartoon B?

▶ What message did the customer *not* receive? Why?

_____

▼ Practice

Think about a recent mix-up or misunderstanding you had with someone. Then answer the questions below.

1. Who was the main speaker (sender)?

2. Who was the main listener (receiver)?

3. What was the misunderstanding?

4. Why wasn't the communication clear?

Rate Your Communication Skills

How well do you **communicate** with other people? How do your communication skills affect the way you do your work? Here is a chance to think about the communication skills you already have and the ones you would like to improve. Read each statement below and check the column that best describes you.

	Already do well	Want to improve
1. I ask questions when I don't understand.	_____	_____
2. To make sure I understand, I repeat what someone else has said in my own words.	_____	_____
3. I notice people's facial expressions (surprised, angry, and so on).	_____	_____
4. I give clear directions.	_____	_____
5. I listen carefully and speak clearly on the phone.	_____	_____
6. My requests are easy to understand.	_____	_____
7. I give good reasons to explain my opinions.	_____	_____
8. I respect other people's right to state their opinions.	_____	_____
9. I respond calmly to criticism.	_____	_____

SHOW IT!

Communication does not rely on words alone. Your **body language**—the way you sit, stand, and move—also sends signals to other people. Your facial expressions send signals, too.

What message is this student sending to her teacher?

What message is this football player sending to the other team?

APPLYING YOUR SKILLS

IN YOUR LIFE

1. Why is clear communication important among family members? Give examples to explain your answer.

_____

_____

2. Why is clear communication important in the workplace? Give examples to explain your answer.

_____

_____

WORKING TOGETHER

Choose a partner to work with. Read the list of jobs below. Discuss with your partner the communication skills these jobs require. Consider each of these categories:

- speaking skills
- listening skills

If possible, think of specific examples based on your own experiences. Write your answers on the lines below. Follow the example.

1. talk-show host _____

_____

2. basketball coach _____

_____

3. office supervisor _____

_____

4. doctor _____

_____

5. janitor _____

_____

6. mayor _____

_____

7. hairstylist _____

_____

8. news reporter _____

_____

What Are You Talking About?

Carl and Lisa work at the Northside Daycare Center. Carl takes care of the three-year-olds, and Lisa takes care of the four-year-olds. Every Monday, during nap time, they discuss their planned activities for the week.

Carl finally got the three-year-olds to sleep. He walked to the back of the room where Lisa was sitting. She was holding a four-year-old girl on her lap. The young girl was crying uncontrollably.

"Lisa, is it a good time to discuss our plans for the week?" asked Carl.

"Sure," said Lisa, rocking the young girl on her lap.

"Well," Carl began, "I've been thinking about a new game we could try. I read it in a book I got from the library . . ."

"Great," said Lisa with her head down. She was trying to get the young girl to stop crying.

"Anyway, I think the book has a lot of ideas we could use. Would you like to read it?" Carl asked.

"Yes, that would be fine. Why don't we talk more about it later?"

A few days later, Carl brought the library book to the daycare center.

"Here's the book I was telling you about." He handed the book to Lisa.

"What book?" asked Lisa. "I don't know what you're talking about."

▼ For Discussion
1. Why did Lisa and Carl have trouble communicating?
2. How would the story be different if Carl had paid attention to Lisa's body language?
3. Why is it important to listen to the words and notice body language at the same time? Give specific examples from your own experiences.

Lesson 1 Summary
- Successful communication occurs when the receiver understands the sender's message.
- People communicate messages by writing, speaking, listening, and reading.
- People also communicate messages through their body language—the way they sit, stand, and move, and the expressions on their faces.
- Communication skills can be learned and practiced.

Communication Strategies

Dr. Martin Luther King, Jr., speaking at a civil rights rally.

President John F. Kennedy delivering a speech during a debate.

Talk About It

- Why do you think the listeners in the audience are paying close attention to the speeches?
- How would you define a good speaker?
- How would you define a good listener?

Active Listening

"I keep telling him what I think, but I can't get through to him."

"She doesn't listen to a word I say."

Have you ever said something like this? Do you ever have trouble listening to messages from other people? Listening seems like an easy skill, but it really requires hard work.

What are your listening habits? Take a few minutes to rate yourself. Read each statement below. Circle *Yes* if it is true for you most of the time. Circle *No* if it is not true for you most of the time.

1. I allow the other person to finish what he or she is saying before I speak.   Yes   No

2. I pay attention even when I don't like the speaker.   Yes   No

3. I easily ignore distractions when I am listening.   Yes   No

4. I can easily remember what other people say to me.   Yes   No

5. I ask the speaker questions when I don't understand something.   Yes   No

6. I look at people when they are talking to me.   Yes   No

Your *Yes* statements show that you already have some active listening habits. In other words, you are involved in the communication process. You take responsibility for understanding the speaker's message.

Reread your *No* statements. What steps could you take to change those listening habits? With practice, you can improve your listening skills.

▼ Practice

Part A

Read each situation below. Then answer the questions.

1. Sylvia is washing dishes while talking on the phone. Her two children are in the next room watching TV. Sylvia can hear them fighting with each other.

Do you think Sylvia is actively listening to her friend on the phone? Why or why not?

2. Gerald is watching the TV news. A reporter is interviewing the mayor about his plans to reform the school system. Gerald dislikes the mayor and didn't vote for him in the last election.

Do you think Gerald will listen to the mayor's plans without judging him? Why or why not?

3. Raul is at a parent-teacher conference at school. His son is having trouble learning, and the teacher is suggesting ways to help him. The teacher uses a term that Raul has never heard, so Raul asks what the term means.

Do you think Raul is actively listening to the teacher? Why or why not?

Part B

Work in small groups. Think of a time when you were speaking and the other person wasn't listening. How did you know that he or she didn't understand your message? How did the person show that he or she wasn't paying attention? Discuss these questions with one another.

Listening Tips

As you read these tips, think about how you can apply them.

DO'S
- **DO** look at the speaker to show you are paying attention.
- **DO** avoid daydreaming.
- **DO** ignore distracting outside noises.
- **DO** ask questions if you are confused.

DON'TS
- **DON'T** rush, interrupt, or finish sentences for the speaker.
- **DON'T** think about what you want to say while the other person is speaking.
- **DON'T** stop paying attention because you disagree with the speaker.

Speaking Tips

Think about some of your conversations with friends, family, or coworkers. When you are listening to someone else, what speaking habits do you appreciate? Finish these sentences:

1. I enjoy listening to a person who _____.
2. I can tell the speaker knows what she's talking about when _____.
3. I can tell the speaker is paying attention to me when _____.

What speaking habits bother you? Finish these sentences:

1. I get impatient with a speaker when _____.
2. I stop paying attention when the speaker _____.
3. I have trouble listening to someone who _____.

What did you discover in the exercise above? You may have found that a speaker's habits affect the way you listen. You can help the other person listen and understand when you send a message. Below are some tips for effective speaking.

Speaking Tips

- **Be clear and brief.** Tell listeners exactly what you want them to know or do.
- **Say what you mean.** Use words listeners will understand.
- **Respond to the listeners.** Do they seem confused by what you said? Are they getting impatient? Give them a chance to ask questions or comment.

▼ Practice

Work in pairs. Take turns speaking to your partner about one of these topics:

- a movie you really liked
- your favorite TV show
- an experience from your job
- a family member you admire

During your short talk, try to follow the speaking tips above.

Speaking at Work

How does speaking to your friends differ from speaking to your coworkers or boss? With friends, you usually don't spend time planning what you will say. However, at your job, sometimes you will need to think carefully *before* you speak. Some of these situations are:

- interviewing for a job
- training a coworker
- discussing a problem with your boss
- sharing opinions at meetings

▶ Add your own examples here:

_____

_____

To help you plan, you may want to write down some short notes. For example, Sheila attends monthly meetings at her office where she and her coworkers discuss their work problems with one another. To prepare for the meetings, Sheila jots down issues she wants to discuss. Study an example of her notes below:

> Problems in office supply room:
> —Remind employees to use sign-out sheet
> —Sign-out sheet keeps track of office supplies

Because she had her notes handy, Sheila was able to report the problems clearly.

SHOW IT!

The picture below shows a hotel housekeeper talking to her boss.

What silent message do you think the boss is sending to the housekeeper? If you were the housekeeper, how would you respond?

▼ Practice

Think of a problem that you have at home or at work. Who should you discuss this problem with? On a separate sheet of paper, write down some issues that you want to discuss with that person. Then, when the time is right, discuss the problem.

▼ Practice

You can do this exercise in one of two ways:

1. Read the story below once or twice and then answer the questions.

OR

2. Find a partner or two in your class. Have one group member read the story below out loud as you follow along. Then answer the questions.

Joe entered Hitech Electronics, hauling his stereo under one arm. It was a busy Saturday morning, and the store was filled with customers. Joe made his way toward the endless line next to the repairs counter. When he finally reached the front of the line, a young woman greeted him.

"How may I help you?" she asked. She looked down and shuffled through a pile of receipts as she waited for Joe to answer.

"Well, see, I need to get my stereo fixed. I had a party a couple of months ago, and some of my friends got pretty wild. Anyway, I think somebody must have bumped into the stereo while it was playing. Or maybe someone spilled food on it, because it doesn't work anymore."

"What seems to be the problem?" the saleswoman asked.

"It makes a funny noise," Joe said. "And the problem started right after that party. Or it could have been the week before, when my brother helped me move into my new apartment."

"OK, but what specifically is the problem?" asked the saleswoman, looking at her watch.

"You know when you're trying to make a tape from a record? Well, on the tape you hear——"

"A background noise?" the saleswoman interrupted. "That's very common. I think I know what's causing the problem. If you leave the stereo here, someone will take a look at it. Then I'll call you about the cost. Your name, please?"

"No, I don't think it's background noise," Joe said. "I think it comes from inside the machine. It sounds like something from outer space."

"Now, that's a really helpful description!" the saleswoman snorted. "Could you get to the point? Other customers are waiting."

1. Was Joe's explanation of the problem helpful? Why or why not?

2. Was the saleswoman a good listener? Give specific reasons for your answer.

3. What caused the communication problem between Joe and the saleswoman? How could each of them have avoided the problem?

APPLYING YOUR SKILLS

IN YOUR LIFE

1. Whom do you talk to when you have a personal problem? Why do you consider that person a good listener?

_____

_____

_____

_____

2. Think of a speaker you admire—a talk-show host, for example, or a political leader, or a preacher. Does the person use the speaking methods discussed in this lesson? If so, give examples of the methods he or she uses.

_____

_____

_____

_____

_____

WORKING TOGETHER

Choose a partner. Each of you will talk about a topic of your choice for two minutes. Your partner will simply listen. As the listener, don't say anything—just listen. Let the speaker know you are listening by nodding your head, smiling, raising your eyebrows, and so on. Then switch roles.

After you finish the activity, discuss the following questions with each other:

• As the speaker, how did you feel knowing that you wouldn't be interrupted? Did you feel as if you should take more time to think about what you were going to say? Did you feel more pressure? Did you feel that the other person was listening, even though she or he wasn't saying anything?

• As the listener, how did you feel about not being allowed to respond? Were you distracted by things you wanted to say? Did you listen more carefully since you didn't have to think about what you would say?

Let Me Tell You About . . .

Ahmed and Leo were finishing washing the floor in the waiting room at Children's Memorial Hospital.

Ahmed: Leo, did you watch that football game on TV last night?

Leo: No, I went out with some friends. We went to a new Chinese restaurant in our neighborhood.

Ahmed: It was so exciting! The two teams were tied, and the game had to go into overtime. I thought my team was going to lose when——

Leo: That sounds great! But let me tell you about what I ordered——

Ahmed: It was the fourth quarter, and my team had only ten yards to go. Then, the quarterback was injured.

Leo: I'm sorry I missed that game, but we had a delicious dinner. It was the first time I tried——

Ahmed: What a game! I couldn't tell who was going to win.

Leo: I guess it really was a great game. Ahmed, I have an idea. Do you like Chinese food? We could go sometime on our night off.

Ahmed: I can't wait until next week's game because the quarterback——

Leo: I wish you would stop talking about football! I don't really know much about football.

Ahmed: If you would just listen to me, I could explain it to you.

▼ For Discussion

1. Are Ahmed and Leo good listeners? Why or why not?
2. Are Ahmed and Leo good speakers? Why or why not?
3. Why is good communication with coworkers important at a job?

Lesson 2 Summary

- Active listeners take responsibility for understanding the speaker's message.
- Speaking on the job requires more planning than speaking with friends.
- Speak clearly and briefly, and respond to listeners' reactions.

Listening to Instructions

Questions for the Doctor

Mrs. Greco had brought her seven-year-old son, Michael, to the doctor.

"How is he?" Mrs. Greco asked.

"Michael is going to be fine in a few days," Dr. Corrigan said. "He's getting over a bad cold. I'll give you some medicine to take care of his remaining symptoms." Dr. Corrigan opened up one of her cabinets.

"Is it OK to give him different medicines at once?" Mrs. Greco asked.

"I want you to give him two teaspoons of cough syrup only at night. It will help him sleep better. The white pills are for his runny nose and headaches——"

"Wait a minute, Dr. Corrigan, this is going to be a lot to remember. I'd better write down your instructions," Mrs. Greco said as she reached into her purse to take out a pen and a small pad of paper.

"Very good—I'll start again. You are to give Michael the cough syrup only at night. It is very strong, and it will help him sleep. The white pills work like aspirin to take away any pain, and they work to dry up his runny nose. Are you getting all this?" Dr. Corrigan asked.

Mrs. Greco nodded her head.

Dr. Corrigan continued: "You can give him one pill before he goes to school and one pill before he goes to bed."

This nurse is listening to the doctor's instructions.

Mrs. Greco repeated the instructions. "OK, that's cough syrup only at night, and one white pill before school and another before bed."

"That's right," Dr. Corrigan smiled.

"So, I only need to give Michael the medicine for about two or three days?"

"Three days should do it. Just remember—if Michael is not better in three days, I want you to call me."

Talk About It

- What techniques did Mrs. Greco use to make sure she would remember Dr. Corrigan's instructions?
- What do you do when someone gives you a list of instructions to follow?

Listening to Instructions

You have been listening to directions or **instructions** all your life. For example, you learned to drive or cook by listening to instructions and watching other people.

▶ What have you recently learned by listening and watching other people?

_____

Earlier, you read about how Mrs. Greco learned to give her son medicine. What are some of the listening skills she used to understand the doctor's instructions?

- **She listened for the main points:**
  - the purpose of the medicine
  - the amount of medicine
  - the times to give the medicine

- **She asked specific questions:**
  - "Is it OK to give him different medicines at once?"
  - "So, I only need to give Michael the medicine for two or three days?"

- **She took notes on the doctor's instructions.**

What's Most Important?

Vince had been driving around in circles for half an hour. He finally decided to ask a man for directions.

Vince: Hey, Mister, how do I get to Route 3 from here?

Man: You go down to the *next stop sign*. Take a *right* there. I think that's Hayes Road. I'm not positive though. But I know it's the next stop sign. Take that right, then go about *three miles* to a "Y" *in the road*. You'll see it because there's a *collapsed barn* right there. But you'll know you've gone too far if you pass a blue house. So *bear right* at the "Y" and that will take you right into Route 3.

Vince: I turn right at the next stop sign and go three miles to the "Y" in the road by the collapsed barn. I bear right and that will take me to Route 3.

> Right at first sign, 3 miles to the Y, bear right.

► What was Vince's goal?

► Which facts did he need in order to accomplish his goal?

► How did Vince make sure that he understood the man?

To be sure you understand instructions, repeat only the most important facts to the speaker. When you listen to instructions, ask yourself these questions:

- What is the goal?

- What are the main points? Which information will help me accomplish the goal?

▼ Practice

Part A
Prepare to tell someone how to get to your home from the school. Make some notes for yourself and practice giving directions.

Part B
Work with a partner. One person will give directions about how to get from one place to another. The other person will listen and then repeat the directions.

What's the Correct Order?

How can you tell when to perform each step of a task? One way is to listen for **clue words**. For example, imagine that you work for a housecleaning service. When you arrive at your job, the owner of the house says, "Today's work should take just a few hours. **First**, I'd like you to defrost the refrigerator. **Next**, clean the oven. **After** that, please mop the floor. Oh, and don't forget to sweep the floor **before** you mop it."

► In what order should you do the steps?

1. _____

2. _____

3. _____

4. _____

The steps go in this order: defrost the refrigerator, clean the oven, sweep the floor, mop the floor. You know this because of clue words: *first, then, after,* and *before.*

Here is a list of clue words you may hear:

first	second	third
next	finally	before
last	after	then

▼ **Communication Tip**

When you listen to instructions, listen for pauses and clue words. These may signal a new step or task.

▼ Practice

Read each set of instructions below and circle the clue words. Then write the order of the steps.

1. "Type up this letter and then make a copy. Wait—before you copy the letter, bring it to me so I can check it and sign it."

2. "Don't forget—all refund slips must be approved by the manager. Have the customer fill out and sign the slip before you show it to the manager."

3. "Bring the boxes of pens out to the front of the store. Then refill the displays. Before you bring the boxes out, check to see which pens don't write and remove them."

4. "Please file these new client contracts. First, place each contract in its own folder. Then, label each folder with the client's name. The last name is written before the first name."

Asking Questions

Sometimes instructions may not make sense to you. You'll probably ask yourself: Did I miss an important point? Were part of the directions unclear? Did the other person leave out some steps?

If you are confused, ask the speaker to explain. Employers are only human. Their instructions may not always be clear or complete. Learn to ask *specific questions*, rather than "Huh?" or "Could you repeat all of that?"

Sometimes you may want to check a specific fact. For example, "Did you say to order 100 or 125 pounds of Parmesan cheese?" Or you may need more information about how to complete the task. For instance, imagine that you are repairing the wiring in a wall. Your supervisor tells you to use 18-gauge wire. In the past, you used that kind of wire for outlets only, not for an entire wiring job.

▶ What question could you ask?

_____

You might ask a question like this: *"Should I use 18-gauge wire for the whole job or just for the outlet?"*

Remember to wait for the speaker to pause before you ask your questions. Try not to interrupt the speaker.

▼ Practice

Jeff Wilson has just taken a job as a short-order cook at The Sandwich Shoppe, a restaurant that specializes in sandwiches. The kitchen stocks a variety of breads and cheeses. Jeff's coworker Paul is giving him instructions for making the day's special double-decker sandwich. Read Paul's instructions and answer the questions.

Paul: OK. First you take three slices of bread. Put one slice of bread flat on the counter. Then layer these items onto it: two slices of cheese, avocado slices, lettuce, tomato, and bean sprouts. Put mayonnaise on the second slice of bread and lay that slice on top of the sandwich. Then cut the sandwich in half and put a toothpick in each half.

1. If you were Jeff, could you follow these instructions? Why or why not?

2. What questions would you ask Paul?

Taking Notes

Gene, Linda's boss, is giving Linda delivery instructions:

> "This order has to get to East Street by 9 A.M. I know it's on the other side of town, but you'd better deliver it first. The only other order that has to get there early is this one on Rivera Street. Well, deliver either the East or Rivera order first. Then, after you deliver those two, just follow the usual route. On second thought, before you do *anything* else, deliver to Mr. Roma on Talbot Street."

> ② East Street
>   or
> ③ Rivera Street
> ④ Regular Route
> ① Talbot Street

Linda had been taking notes as Gene was talking. She hadn't numbered the steps until Gene was done speaking.

She read the order of deliveries back to Gene: "Talbot Street first, then East or Rivera, then the regular route."

Like Linda, you may want to take brief **notes** about how to do a task or what tasks need to be done. Note taking helps you remember what someone has told you.

Here are some tips for note taking:

- Focus on main points.
- Listen for clue words.
- Write the information down as short steps.
- Number the steps in correct order.
- Read the instructions back to the speaker.
- Ask specific questions if necessary.
- Write down any corrections or added instructions.

▼ Practice

Work with a partner. One person should read the following instructions aloud while the other takes notes. Follow the tips for note taking. Ask questions if you are unsure of the directions. Then switch roles.

> "Turn the machine on and let the water run. Put powdered detergent in this top basket. But wait until the machine fills with water before adding the powdered detergent. Then the powder will dissolve completely. Remember to turn the dial to the correct water temperature at the very beginning. By the way, the fabric softener goes in when the rinse light comes on."

APPLYING YOUR SKILLS

IN YOUR LIFE

1. When do you need to follow directions at home, school, or work? How do you make sure that you correctly understand the information?

_____

_____

_____

_____

_____

2. Think about a time when you had to listen to directions. What skills from this lesson did you use? What skills have you learned in this lesson that you can apply in the future? Give examples to explain your answers.

_____

_____

_____

_____

_____

WORKING TOGETHER

One person should read the orders below. With their books closed, the rest of the group should write down the order on a separate piece of paper and then check their orders against the following:

I'd like to place an order. I'd like a large order of chicken wings, very hot. Also, a medium pizza with everything except anchovies and mushrooms. And a large pizza with extra cheese, half with olives and half with mushrooms.

I'd like to place an order. A submarine sandwich, hold the lettuce, and a large coffee.

I'd like to place an order. I'd like two house salads, one with French dressing and the other with Italian. Also, a large deep-dish spinach pizza and two medium iced teas.

PROBLEM SOLVER ▼ | I Think I Understand

It was Wayne's first day of work. Sofia, the assistant manager, was showing him how to operate the cash register.

"Wayne, watch how I ring up this sale," Sofia said as she rang up some purchases for a customer.

Wayne watched carefully but did not say anything.

"Now, that sale wasn't hard because the customer used cash. Sometimes, the customer will write a check. We only take checks if the customer can show two forms of identification. One form must be a major credit card, and the other can be a driver's license." Sofia looked at Wayne to see if he understood. Wayne was nodding his head.

"We also accept credit cards. We take MasterCard and Visa but not Discover and American Express."

"OK," Wayne said, "I think I understand everything."

"Good. Here comes a customer. I'll watch you ring up the sale."

Wayne nervously nodded his head. He took the customer's item and began punching in the numbers of the price. He asked the customer how she would be paying. She said that she wanted to write a check. Wayne then asked for two forms of identification. When the woman took out her American Express card, Wayne said, "I'm sorry, but I can't accept American Express."

"No, Wayne, any major credit card will do for a check. She just can't *pay* with American Express," Sofia said. "Here—I'll finish this sale. After I'm done, we can go over it again."

▼ For Discussion

1. Why did Wayne have problems with the sale?
2. How could Wayne have remembered the steps involved in ringing up a sale?
3. Think of a time when you received a long set of instructions. How did you make sure you could understand and remember them?

Lesson 3 Summary

- Focus on the main points.
- Listen for the order of the steps.
- Repeat the information to the speaker.
- Ask questions if you don't understand or need more information.
- Take brief notes if necessary.

Giving Directions

What To Do About Food Poisoning

"Here's Henry Chang, from the City Health Department," said Sylvia Alvarez, an anchorwoman for the Channel 20 News.

"Thank you, Sylvia. Tonight, I'd like to warn the public about our recent outbreak of food poisoning. I want people to be careful with the food they bring home from the supermarket.

"I'm here in the studio kitchen to talk to you about chicken.

"When preparing chicken, please follow these steps:

Cooks must be alert to the dangers of food poisoning.

- Defrost the chicken in the refrigerator. Do not keep it at room temperature.

- Rinse chicken in cold water.

- Wash any surface that the raw chicken will touch with soap and water—this means the sink, cutting board, and any utensils.

- Make sure the chicken is fully cooked. Do not eat chicken if the meat is pink.

(Henry demonstrates each action.)
"If you have any questions about how to prevent food poisoning, please call the City Health Department."

"Thank you, Henry," said Sylvia. "The City Health Department also warns us about food poisoning in restaurants." Sylvia begins to read the slide that is across the screen.

- Check the chicken you eat at restaurants.

- Make sure the chicken meat is fully cooked. If it is not, ask the waiter or waitress to take it back to the kitchen.

Talk About It

- Are Henry's directions clear? Why or why not?
- How is Henry's demonstration of the directions helpful?
- What other instructions might you hear on the news?

Explaining a Task

Think about a time when you taught someone how to do something. Maybe you taught your sister to do a card trick or showed your child how to throw a football or baseball. Maybe you showed a stranger how to use a vending machine or a copying machine. Everyone has knowledge and skills to share with other people.

What do you do to explain a task? You probably picture yourself doing the task, from start to finish.

Before you start to give instructions, get a clear idea of what needs to be done. Picture the task or tasks. If you can't remember all of the steps, ask another person for information. If there are written instructions, reread them.

▼ Practice

Write instructions for doing two of these tasks:

Sharpening a pencil
Pumping gas into a car
Parallel parking
Replacing a burnt-out
  light bulb

Washing dishes
Making instant coffee
Placing a long distance
  phone call
Choosing ripe fruit at
  the supermarket

1. Task: _____

  Instructions: _____

_____

_____

_____

2. Task: _____

  Instructions: _____

_____

_____

_____

Putting the Steps In Order

Could you imagine a child following these instructions the first time she brushed her teeth?

> "OK, to brush your teeth, start with your front teeth. Put the toothbrush in your mouth. Oh, before that, open the tube of toothpaste and put some toothpaste on your brush. When you're all done, rinse your mouth with water, but don't do that until you have brushed the top and bottom teeth . . ."

▼ **Communication Tip**

Plan your instructions by picturing the task and ordering the steps.

When you explain a task to others, break the task or job into short steps. Then plan the order of the steps. **Time order** is a good way of organizing steps. In other words, you should give the steps in the order they have to be done. Remember the time order words from page 20: *first, second, before, after,* and so on.

Recipes are good models for giving instructions. A recipe lists all the ingredients you need for the dish so you can assemble them ahead of time. You won't get to the middle of the cooking and find that you don't have a key ingredient. Also, a recipe breaks the cooking down into steps, according to time order.

▼ Practice

Part A
Think of a task you can do easily. Then prepare to teach another person to do the task. First picture the task. Break it down into steps and write the steps in time order.

Part B
Break down this recipe into short steps. Then work with a partner and explain the steps aloud.

APPETIZER

Zucchini and Sesame Seeds

Slice a medium zucchini and an onion. Then heat 3 tablespoons of oil in a heavy skillet. Let the oil get very hot, then sauté the onions and zucchini in the oil for 5 to 10 minutes. Stir the mixture a few times so it doesn't stick. When the onions and zucchini are tender, add 2 tablespoons of sesame seeds and 1 tablespoon of soy sauce and stir. Serve it right away.

Presenting Instructions

Once you've pictured the task and put the steps in order, you're ready to give instructions.

- **Set the stage.** Tell the listeners what you'll be explaining. Let your listeners know what to expect.

  Examples:

  "First, I'll just tell you what each of the controls is for. Then I'll tell you how to use this machine."

  "I'm going to show you where we put our tools."

  "I want to show you how to empty the money from the soda machine."

- **Give word clues.** Use word clues to show that you are moving on to a new step or task.

  Examples:

"Next,"	"The second step is . . ."
"Finally,"	"When you finish . . ."
"After you do this . . ."	"At the same time . . ."

- **Speak clearly and slowly.** Don't rush. Remember, you are introducing new information to your listeners. Give them time to understand it.

- **Check the listeners' understanding.** Pause now and then between steps in case there are questions.

  Examples:

  "Are you with me so far?"

  "Do you have any questions?"

- **Give encouragement.** Think about how *you* feel when you are trying to learn a new task. Learning new information or skills can be difficult. Be sure to encourage the listeners along the way.

  Examples:

  "This may seem complicated, but you'll get the hang of it."

  "It just takes some practice. Take it slowly at first."

Showing What to Do

People learn in many different ways. Most people learn best by seeing, touching, or even hearing. Can you *show* what you are teaching? Study the examples below.

Task	Teaching Method	
How to throw a basketball	Demonstrate with your hands and body	
How to operate a machine	Demonstrate using the machine	

SHOW IT!

Look at the pictures below.

How do TV demonstrations help TV viewers learn?

▼ Practice

Part A

At home, watch a TV program that shows you how to do something: cook, make simple home repairs, or exercise, for example. (These types of programs are usually featured on educational channels or cable channels.) As you watch the show, answer the following questions:

1. What is the title of the TV program?

   _____

2. What task or skill is the program presenting?

   _____

3. How does the person on the program *show* the audience how to do the skill or task?

   _____

Part B

Break up into pairs. Keep your hands behind your back or in your pockets for this practice. Now, without using your hands, tell your partner how to do one of these activities:

1. Feed a baby a bottle

2. Lift a heavy box without hurting your back

3. Shampoo someone else's hair

4. Tie a shoelace

5. Shuffle a deck of cards

Now give instructions using your hands.

APPLYING YOUR SKILLS

IN YOUR LIFE

1. Describe a task you have taught someone who was learning it for the first time. What did you do to make the task easy to understand?

_____

_____

_____

_____

_____

2. Did someone ever misunderstand your directions or instructions? If so, whose fault was it—yours or the listener's? On the lines below, briefly describe what happened.

_____

_____

_____

_____

_____

WORKING TOGETHER

Part A

Bring in a product from home that has directions on it. During the next class, choose a partner. Tell the other person how to use the product. The listener should make faces or gestures showing understanding or confusion.

Part B

Work in pairs. Each of you will take turns telling your partner how to use one of the items below. Don't assume that the other person already knows how to operate it. Follow the guidelines for presenting instructions on page 28.

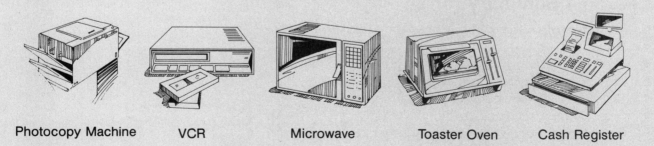

Photocopy Machine   VCR   Microwave   Toaster Oven   Cash Register

PROBLEM SOLVER

Two Sides of the Story

Phil's Story

Phil was very angry. He had just been hired by the Kitchen Company. The boss had told Fred to train Phil. Phil was tired of Fred always telling him how to do everything. He didn't mind that Fred told him again today how to use the power saw and the drill. He didn't mind that Fred told him how to cut a 45-degree angle, though Phil had already cut two boards himself. After all, Fred had been installing kitchen cabinets for years. But when Fred tried to show him how to sweep the floor without raising too much sawdust, Phil lost his temper. He could sweep a floor. He didn't need Fred telling him how to do that too!

Fred's Story

Fred had been feeling very pleased. Phil was doing very well, and Fred liked working with him. Phil was eager to learn new skills. Fred liked showing him how to do things. Fred had shown him how to use the power saw and the drill. He explained how to cut the boards at a 45-degree angle. In fact, he had even shown Phil his method for sweeping so as not to raise much dirt and sawdust. But now Phil was mad at him, and he didn't know why. Everything was going along just fine and then all of a sudden, when Fred reached for the broom, Phil stormed off.

▼ **For Discussion**

1. Do you think Phil has a right to be angry at Fred? Give reasons to explain your answer.
2. If you were Fred, what would you say or do?
3. Sometimes, new employees already have work experience. How should their experience affect their job training?

Lesson 4 Summary

- Prepare yourself by going over the task.
- Break the task into short steps.
- Tell your listeners what you are going to explain.
- Present your instructions clearly.
- *Show* how to do the task if possible.
- Notice how they react to what you say. If you think they don't understand, stop and check.

Using the Telephone

Is My Car Ready Yet?

Raymond Sanchez works as a car mechanic at Newman's Garage. As usual, he had just gotten under a car when the telephone rang. Raymond finally answered the phone on the tenth ring.

Raymond: Newman's Garage.

Customer: This is Larry Soto. I brought in the '87 Ford Bronco with the muffler problem. Are you finished fixing it yet?

Raymond: What did you say? It's really noisy in here. I didn't hear you.

Customer (*speaking louder*): The name's Soto and I'm calling about my '87 Bronco. Have you already put in the new muffler?

Raymond: John Rice, the other mechanic, is just starting the job now.

Customer: Well, could you tell him to check the brakes, too?

Raymond: Yeah, sure.

Raymond was so busy thinking about the car he was fixing that he forgot to tell John about the phone call.

At noon, the customer called Newman's Garage again and spoke to John.

Like Raymond, this mechanic is engrossed in his work.

Customer: Is my car ready yet?

John: All set.

Customer: So the brakes were OK?

John: (*confused*) What do you mean? I put in a new muffler.

Customer: That's right, but I talked to the other mechanic this morning about my brakes. He said he'd tell you to check them.

John: Sorry about that, but I never got the message. I won't have a chance to look at them until later this afternoon.

Customer: (*angry*) Forget it. I need the car now. I'll take it to another garage.

Talk About It

- Have you ever forgotten to deliver a phone message? What happened?
- What are the advantages of using the phone to take care of business? What are the disadvantages?

Improving Phone Skills

You've probably been using the phone most of your life. Yet you may still want to sharpen your telephone listening and speaking skills.

When you are talking face-to-face, you use your hands, your face, your voice, your entire body to communicate. But when you use the phone, you can't see body language or the look on the other person's face. So using the phone requires very clear speaking and active, focused listening.

When you talk on the phone at work, you may have to pay even more attention if you are talking to strangers. Maybe the other person doesn't speak clearly. Or maybe the caller has an accent that you are not used to. Concentrate very carefully. If you don't understand, ask the person to repeat what he or she said.

Have you called a doctor's office, a government office, a store, or the telephone or utility company? These were business calls. Most likely, the people who answered the phone spoke in a businesslike manner.

▶ How did you speak and listen during these calls? Would you speak to friends and relatives the same way?

▼ Practice

Think about one personal call and one business call you have made recently. Write down some of the differences here:

	Personal Call	Business Call
Who I called		
Preparation for the call		
What I talked about		
Speaking style (informal, businesslike)		

Answering the Phone at Work

▶ Think of one of those business calls you made. What did the other person say when he or she answered the phone?

_____

People in the workplace usually say the name of the business or office:

"Hello, MacDonald's Farm and Garden Shop."

"Hello, Consumer Affairs Office."

"Good morning, Dr. Freeborough's office."

Some businesses have a receptionist who answers the phone and connects callers with a department. When a person answers the department phone, he or she says the name of the department and his or her name:

"Service Department, Mark Hatch speaking."

"Children's Clothes, Ms. O'Reilly."

"Customer Service, this is Mr. Gorman."

Calling Your Place of Work

Have you ever made plans to meet a friend who didn't show up or arrived late? How did you react?

Employers expect you to show up at work. They also expect you to be on time. If you are sick or are going to be late, be sure to call your employer. Talk to your immediate **supervisor**. Explain why you will be late or absent. If you will be late, say when you will get to work.

▼ Communication Tip
Avoid smoking or eating during a business call.

▼ Practice

Part A
1. What situations might cause you to be late to work?

_____

2. What should you do if you are late?

_____

Part B
Choose a partner. One of you will be the employee, and the other, the boss. As the employee, call your boss and tell him or her that you will be late or that you won't be in at all. Then switch roles.

Listening to Take a Message

You may need to take a message if someone isn't available to take a call. Taking a message requires careful listening and some writing. When you take a message, write down the key information:

- the caller's name and number
- the time and date of the call
- the purpose of the call (if appropriate)
- the time when the caller can be reached

Below, Miguel, a clerk, takes a message for Bob Filipo, his supervisor.

(Two volunteers could read aloud the phone conversation.) As you read or listen to the dialogue, think about the phone skills needed for the conversation.

The phone rang in the parts department early Tuesday afternoon. Miguel answered.

Miguel: Filipo Paints.

Mr. Daniels: Is Bob Filipo in? This is Roland Daniels at Rainbow Trucking.

Miguel: He's out back right now. May I take a message?

Mr. Daniels: Yeah, all right. Just ask him to call me. My number's 555-3096.

Miguel: That was 555-3095?

Mr. Daniels: No, 555-3096.

Miguel: 555-3096.

Mr. Daniels: That's right.

Miguel: And what did you say your name was?

Mr. Daniels: Roland Daniels. And tell him I'll only be here until four. And then all day tomorrow.

Miguel: OK, Mr. Daniels—before four or all day tomorrow. I'll give Mr. Filipo your message. Good-bye.

Miguel wrote the information on a message form and left it on Mr. Filipo's desk.

▶ What skills did Miguel use in taking the phone message?

_____

_____

_____

► What phone skills do you think Miguel could improve?

_____

_____

Miguel showed he had some good skills. He offered to take a message. He repeated the phone number to be sure it was correct. He addressed the caller by name at the end. He also repeated the entire message back to Mr. Daniels. However, he didn't ask Mr. Daniels, "May I ask your reason for calling?" As a result, Bob Filipo won't know *why* Mr. Daniels called.

▼ Practice

As you read the dialogue below, write questions for the receptionist to ask. Use the clues in the boxes on the left.

Receptionist:	Bryant's Hospital Supply.
Ms. Romero:	May I speak to Ms. Shaw?
Receptionist:	I'm sorry, she's out right now. May I take a message?
Ms. Romero:	Yes. This is Maria Romero at Forest Park Hospital.

Ask to spell last name	**1. Receptionist:**	_____
	Ms. Romero:	R-o-m-e-r-o.
Ask for a phone number	**2. Receptionist:**	_____
	Ms. Romero:	555-1732.
Repeat number	**3. Receptionist:**	_____
	Ms. Romero:	Could you tell Ms. Shaw to call me tomorrow?
Ask for best time to call	**4. Receptionist:**	_____
	Ms. Romero:	Anytime after 10:30.
	Receptionist:	Thank you. I'll give her the message.

Using a Message Form

A telephone message form helps you to get all of the important information. The terms printed on the form remind you to ask for the information you need.

▼ Practice

Read the dialogue below. Fill out the message form based on the dialogue. Use the current date and time, and sign your name on the form.

Receptionist: Ace Credit Union. May I help you?

Caller: May I speak with Anthony Lewis?

Receptionist: I'm sorry. He's gone for the day. May I take a message?

Caller: Yes. This is James Pixler returning his call.

Receptionist: Could you spell your last name, please?

Caller: P-i-x-l-e-r.

Receptionist: And your phone number?

Caller: It's area code 713, 555-7489.

Receptionist: I'll give Mr. Lewis the message.

MESSAGE

FOR _____   DATE _____

FROM _____   TIME _____ A.M. / P.M.

PHONE NUMBER _____
             AREA CODE   NUMBER   EXT.

MESSAGE _____

_____

_____

_____

_____

                                                SIGNED _____

APPLYING YOUR SKILLS

IN YOUR LIFE

Answer these questions about your own phone habits.

1. How long does your average phone call last? _____

2. Do you do other things while you are talking on the phone? _____

3. Do you say "what?" or "huh?" a lot? _____

4. Does the other person often ask you to repeat what you said?_____

5. How do you let the other person know you are listening? _____

6. How do you know if the other person is listening? _____

_____

WORKING TOGETHER

With a partner, take turns making a phone call in which you must leave a message. The other person will fill out the message form below.

```
┌─────────────────────────────────────────────────────┐
│              IMPORTANT MESSAGE                        │
│                                                       │
│  FOR _____│
│                                            A.M.       │
│  DATE _____  TIME _____ P.M.      │
│                                                       │
│  M _____│
│                                                       │
│  OF _____│
│                                                       │
│  PHONE _____│
│        AREA CODE         NUMBER          EXTENSION    │
│  ┌──────────────────┬──┬────────────────────┬──┐      │
│  │ TELEPHONED       │  │ PLEASE CALL        │  │      │
│  ├──────────────────┼──┼────────────────────┼──┤      │
│  │ CAME TO SEE YOU  │  │ WILL CALL AGAIN    │  │      │
│  ├──────────────────┼──┼────────────────────┼──┤      │
│  │ RETURNED YOUR    │  │ URGENT             │  │      │
│  │ CALL             │  │                    │  │      │
│  └──────────────────┴──┴────────────────────┴──┘      │
│                                                       │
│  MESSAGE _____│
│                                                       │
│  _____│
│                                                       │
│  _____│
│                                                       │
│  _____│
│                                                       │
│  _____│
│                                                       │
│  SIGNED _____│
└─────────────────────────────────────────────────────┘
```

PROBLEM SOLVER

Too Many Calls

"Ed, telephone call," Emily shouted across the room.

Ed looked up from the order he was working on. He looked around the room to see if Lenore, their supervisor, was anywhere in the room nearby. She had spoken to him earlier in the week about getting too many personal calls at work.

Lenore was not around, so Ed hurried to the phone.

"Hello," he said.

"Hi, Ed, guess who this is," a man's voice said.

"I don't know, and I don't have time for games," Ed answered.

"Hey, don't jump down my throat. This is Emmett. I just wanted to see how you are. I haven't seen you at softball practice in a few weeks."

"I'm sorry," Ed said. "But I'm not supposed to take personal calls here." Just then Lenore walked in.

"I gotta go, Emmett. I'll call you. Bye." Ed hung up the phone and hurried back to his work table.

"Ed," Lenore said as she came over to his work table, "I see you were on the phone again."

"I didn't make the call, Lenore. I hardly ever call out. I can't help it if people call me here."

"Well, you need to work something out with your friends. Every time you get called away from your work, you lose time. And you are more likely to make a mistake on an order. What can we do about all these calls? Is there some way I can help you?"

▼ For Discussion

1. How can Ed handle this situation with his supervisor and with the people he knows?
2. Do you think Lenore was being fair? Why or why not?
3. Do you think it is acceptable to make phone calls from work? When? For what reasons?
4. If your boss said you could receive emergency phone calls only, what situations would you count as an emergency? List them.

Lesson 5 Summary

- The phone skills you use at work are different from those you use at home.
- Include this information when you take or leave a phone message:
  - date
  - time
  - caller's name and number
  - short message

Getting Information

The Survey

Lupe had just started working at the new shopping mall in her neighborhood. She worked for the customer assistance office. During her first week, Lupe's supervisor gave her a list of questions called a market survey. She would ask customers these questions as they were leaving the mall.

(*Lupe, holding a clipboard in her arms, approached her first customer, a man in his fifties.*)

Lupe: Excuse me, sir. I'm doing a survey. Would you please answer a few questions?

Man: Yes.

Lupe: Thank you. First, what stores did you shop in today?

Man: I went to the jewelry store.

Lupe: What was your purpose? Buying for yourself? Buying a gift? Returning an item? Just browsing?

Man: I bought a gift for my wife.

Lupe: Did someone help you?

Man: Yes.

Market researchers ask questions to get information.

Lupe: How did the salesperson treat you?

Man: He was very nice. He asked me what I was looking for and showed me many things.

Lupe: Why do you shop here?

Man: I shop here because there are so many stores to choose from. Also, I live only ten minutes away.

(*Lupe thanked the man and walked over to another customer.*)

Talk About It

● Why do you think Lupe asked these questions?
● Why is asking questions a good way to get information?
● Have you ever answered questions on a survey? If so, give some examples of the questions.

What Do You Need To Know?

Study each line drawing below.

What questions do you think the police officer is asking the woman?

What questions do you think the reporter is asking the rock star?

What questions do you think the doctor is asking her patient?

What questions do you think the new employee is asking his boss?

All these people need information to do their jobs. Asking questions is one way of getting that information.

Asking Questions

Notice the words that begin each of the following sentences:

- *Who* could help me fill out my income tax form?
- *What* kind of training does a bank teller need?
- *Where* can I register to vote?
- *When* will the new community center open?
- *Why* are gas prices going up?
- *How* do I apply for United States citizenship?

The first five questions start with the words *who, what, where, when,* and *why.* Try to ask questions that start with these words and the word *how.* Then you'll be able to get the facts or help you need.

At work, you will have questions about how to do your job. Most employers welcome these questions. Asking questions shows that you are interested in doing a good job.

▼ **Communication Tips**

- Ask your question after the speaker is finished talking. You may find that the speaker was just about to tell you what you wanted to know. By interrupting with a question, you might break the speaker's train of thought.
- If possible, write down the question so you will remember to ask it.

▼ Practice

Think of something you are learning at home, school, or work. Then write six questions about the task. Study the example below as a model.

Example:

Task: Learning about the company's policy of paying workers' educational costs.

_____Who_____ is able to receive money for school?

_____What_____ kinds of courses can I take?

_____Where_____ are classes held?

_____When_____ must I notify my boss about my plans to take a course?

_____Why_____ do I need college classes to get a promotion?

_____How_____ will taking a class affect my work schedule?

Types of Questions

Some questions are a little trickier to ask. They usually start with *why*. Some *why* questions are simply requests for more information. They show that you are interested in knowing as much as you can about your work. For instance, a painter might ask a coworker these questions:

- "Why did you use paint rollers this time but paint brushes on that last job?"

- "Why did that wallpaper bubble up?"

Many employers welcome this type of question. If you understand the reason for doing things a certain way, you will be able to solve a lot of work problems yourself.

Sometimes a *yes* or *no* answer or a short answer gives you the information you need in a hurry. Other kinds of questions require the other person to offer more information. Here are some examples.

1. Did you like the movie? (*yes* or *no* question)

2. What did you think of the movie? (opinion question)

▼ Practice

Read the script below. Then answer the questions on a separate sheet of paper.

> **Gail:** How may I help you today?
> **Customer:** I'm looking for a birthday present for my father, but I'm not sure what I want.
> **Gail:** Would you like to look at shirts or sweaters? Or maybe a tie?
> **Customer:** Maybe a shirt.
> **Gail:** Well, here are a few of our bestselling sport shirts. What do you think of these?
> **Customer:** I think my father would probably like this blue knit shirt. Blue is his favorite color, and he could wear it to work. I don't like the other shirts much. My father never wears those styles.

1. Which of Gail's questions asks for specific information?

2. Which of Gail's questions asks for an opinion?

3. Why does a sales clerk need to know how to ask customers different types of questions? Give examples from your own experiences as a customer.

Who Can Answer Your Question?

Sometimes it takes guesswork to figure out who has the information you need. At work, you want to find the answers as quickly as possible. To find the person who can help you, first ask yourself these questions:

- **"Who is most likely to have the information?"** Start with people whose jobs are similar to yours. Maybe a coworker has done this same task. Maybe he or she was at the same meeting where the information was stated. If you're fairly sure that only the supervisor can answer the question, ask him or her first.

- **"Who has the time to answer my question?"** Someone who is very busy may not have time to talk to you right away. Can another person easily answer the question? Can the question wait?

▼ Practice

Choose which person to talk to in each situation. Then, discuss your answers with others. There may be more than one "right" answer.

1. Chris fell at work and broke her arm. She doesn't know whether health insurance or her workers' compensation will pay her medical bills. She should ask

   a. the personnel office

   b. her supervisor

   c. the health insurance representative

   d. her doctor

2. Rob wants to know how to apply for a different job at the company where he works. He should ask

   a. the personnel office

   b. his supervisor

   c. the supervisor of the new job

   d. a coworker

Getting Information by Phone

Making phone calls is another way to get information. Suppose you are moving into a new apartment. You might call different moving companies to find out their rates.

► What other questions would you ask the moving companies?

Getting important information over the phone will then help you decide which moving company to use.

At work, you may also make phone calls to get information. You may want to plan your phone conversation. Study the chart and sample script below.

> ### ▼ Communication Tip
> When you need to get information by phone, keep these handy:
> - paper and pencils
> - list of questions
> - calendar or datebook
> - bill, invoice, or letter

Questions to Ask Yourself	Sample Script
How will you introduce yourself?	"Hello, my name is Joseph Lehman. I'm calling from Rathbone Office Supply."
Who are you calling?	"I'd like to speak to Jill Goldsmith."
Why are you calling?	"I have a question about an order I placed."
What background information should you give?	"We ordered one gray file cabinet. The catalog number is 2451. It's been five weeks and the cabinet hasn't arrived."
What questions do you need answered?	"Has the cabinet been shipped yet?" "When should we expect it?"

▼ Practice

What items would you want to have handy when you make each of these calls?

1. Calling the information operator for a phone number
2. Calling the utility company with a question about your bill
3. Calling a mail order company to place an order
4. Calling a company about a job advertised in the paper

APPLYING YOUR SKILLS

IN YOUR LIFE

Think of a home, school, or work situation for which you need more information. Use the script on page 46 as an example.

1. Describe the situation briefly:

_____

_____

_____

2. Who will you contact?

_____

3. What background information will you give?

_____

4. What questions will you ask?

_____

_____

_____

5. What action will you take after you get the information you need?

_____

_____

WORKING TOGETHER

Break up into small groups. If possible, each group should have at least one person who has worked. Ask that person how he or she gets information at work. If most of you have worked before, then ask each other specific questions about your jobs and workplaces. Remember, the goal of the group is to share information. Notice how others answer the different questions.

Who Was that Stranger?

Mr. Malick arrived home from work around seven o'clock. He waved at Dahlia, the security guard.

When Mr. Malick stepped off the elevator onto his floor, he saw a young man standing in front of the stairwell door. The young man saw Mr. Malick watching him and then went down the stairs.

Mr. Malick hurried into his apartment. He phoned Dahlia.

"Hello Dahlia, this is Mr. Malick in apartment 10-B. I just saw a strange young man on my floor!" Mr. Malick was talking very quickly.

"Mr. Malick, slow down, I can hardly understand you. I want to ask you some questions about the stranger."

"OK," said Mr. Malick.

"Now, you say you saw the man go down the stairwell?"

"Yes, that's right," Mr. Malick said.

"What's so strange about that?" Dahlia asked.

"Well, I live on the *tenth* floor. Most people take the elevator."

"I guess you're right," she said. "Have you ever seen this man before?"

"No, never. I know everyone on my floor."

"Maybe he was just visiting someone?" Dahlia suggested.

"No, I don't think so. He would have taken the elevator if he was just visiting."

"Maybe you're right," she agreed. "Well, I think I have enough information to make a report. Thank you."

▼ For Discussion

1. Does Dahlia have enough information to make a report to her supervisor? Do you think she will find out who the stranger was?
2. Do you think Dahlia is asking good questions?
3. What questions would you have asked if you were Dahlia?

Lesson 6 Summary

- Ask questions beginning with *who, what, where, when, why,* and *how.*
- A question with a *yes* or *no* answer helps you get specific information quickly.
- Plan ahead for the phone calls that you make to get information.

Making and Responding to Requests

Who Will I Help?

"You're going to have to give me a hand tomorrow," Jim said to his friend Bo. "I have to pick up some garden supplies, and you're the guy with the truck! Come by and pick me up at eight."

"Maybe I have other plans," Bo said tensely.

"Listen, when you have a truck, you have to expect that you're going to do some hauling for other people," Jim answered. "Don't be so selfish. I'll see you at eight o'clock. Don't be late. I want to get to the market and beat the crowds."

"You're not listening. Don't tell me what to do," Bo said.

"OK, OK, you don't even have to get up. Just let me use your truck for a few hours. Leave it with me tonight and you can pick it up tomorrow."

Bo shook his head. "Sorry, Jim," he said as he walked away.

Bo had gone only a few steps when George called to him from across the street. "Hey, Bo, can you wait a minute?"

Bo stopped and waited for George. "Bo, I wondered if you have any time this weekend to help me move a few pieces of furniture?"

Jim was still standing there. He snarled, "Bo won't help. He just turned me down."

If you owned a pickup truck, what might people request from you?

Bo started to answer, but George kept talking. "There's nothing too heavy. I know everyone probably keeps asking you for help because you have a truck. But you don't need to lift anything. My brother can help with that. You name a time that's good for you. And I'll be glad to pay you for the gas, too."

"Sure, George. I could probably help you tomorrow morning," Bo said, looking right at Jim.

Talk About It

- Compare Jim's and George's ways of asking for a favor. Why do you think Bo agreed to help George but not Jim?
- Do you ever think it is necessary to make demands?

Making Requests

Do you ever ask other people to do things for you? For example, have you ever asked your mother to babysit for your children? Have you ever asked a friend to give you a ride?

People often ask other people for help. It is a normal part of human relationships. It is also an important communication skill. Most people respond well to **requests** that are made clearly and in a friendly tone of voice.

Tips for Making Requests

- **Asking rather than demanding.**
  Instead of: "You'll have to help me out tomorrow. I have to leave early for a doctor's appointment."
  Ask: "Could you come in a half-hour early tomorrow? I have a doctor's appointment. I'd really appreciate it!"

- **Not trying to make the other person feel guilty.**
  Instead of: "If you were really my friend, you would give me a ride."
  Ask: "I need a ride to my parents' house tonight. Could you drive me over?"

- **Wording your request to get a specific response rather than a vague promise.**
  Instead of: "Can I talk to you later about . . ."
  Ask: "*When* can I talk to you about . . ."

- **For *sensitive* requests, suggesting what you would like to have happen.**
  Instead of: "You are so loud! You'll wake up the kids."
  Say: "You and Joe might be more comfortable talking in the kitchen. Then you won't have to be concerned with waking up the children."

- **Asking in a pleasant tone of voice.**

- **Giving as much advance notice as possible, so the other person can plan.**

▼ Practice

Rewrite these requests using the tips above. Use a separate sheet of paper.

1. You'll have to help me with the groceries.

2. Turn that stereo down! You're waking up the neighborhood.

3. If you don't help me finish this job, I'll get in trouble.

4. I need to talk to you sometime. The freezer isn't working.

5. Hey, type this letter for me!

The Other Person's Response

It is polite to thank someone who does as you request or gives you the information you ask for. People always appreciate a thank-you.

What if you need help and the other person is busy? If you need an answer right away, thank that person and then ask someone else. Otherwise, if the request can wait, ask when the other person will have time to help you.

▼ **Communication Tip**
Treat other people with respect when asking for help.

▼ Practice

Write a request for each situation below. Discuss your answers with the rest of the class.

1. You're a customer in a car parts store, and you'd like the clerk to help you find a distributor cap for your car.

   _____

   _____

2. You'd like your supervisor, Ron, to show you how to fill out a form. Ron is busy and won't be able to help you right away.

   _____

   _____

3. You're a receptionist. You'd like a coworker, Winston, to answer the phone for five minutes while you go to the bathroom.

   _____

   _____

4. You work in a fast-food restaurant. A customer is talking too quickly and you'd like him to slow down.

   _____

   _____

5. Your roommate is on her way to the kitchen. You'd like her to get you a glass of juice.

   _____

   _____

Responding to Requests

At work, you are likely to get requests from coworkers, your boss, and clients or customers. You form a different relationship with each of these people. How should you respond to their requests?

Requests from Coworkers

When coworkers ask you for help, think about these questions:

- Do I have the information?

- Do I have time? Can I do what they are asking and still get all of my work done?

- Is the request reasonable, or are they taking advantage of me? Do they usually ask for favors rather than do things themselves?

If you agree to a request, you should say so clearly. Let your coworkers know that you understand what they are asking. And let them know what to expect from you. How does Roger respond to Lynn's request in the following example?

> **Lynn:** Roger, do you have any time to help me get some letters typed?
>
> **Roger:** Sure, Lynn, I can help you as soon as I finish filing these reports.

If you cannot help someone, you have the right to say no, as Roger does below. Notice how Roger politely turns down Lynn's request:

> **Roger:** Sorry—I can't help you out today, Lynn. I have to get my filing done.

▼ Practice

Think of a situation in which a friend or coworker refused your request. Briefly describe the situation. How did you feel when the other person said no? How did you get the help you needed?

Requests from Your Boss

Sometimes bosses give orders in the form of requests. They're not really asking you if you want to do something, though. They're telling you in a polite way:

> **Boss:** Bill, do you want to clean up this spill?

The boss wants Bill to do more than just say "yes." He expects him to start mopping right away.

► How do you respond when your boss asks you to do a new task?

If you can do the task right away, let your boss know. Ask questions about information you don't understand.

Sometimes your boss's request may conflict with other work you're supposed to do. If this happens, let the boss know. You might have to ask which task to do first.

You also have the right to say no to unfair requests. You aren't required to do special favors or tasks that have nothing to do with your job.

► Can you think of examples of unreasonable requests?

▼ Practice

Part A
In the empty speech balloon, write what you think this employee should say to her boss.

Part B
Suppose your boss asked you to do personal errands, such as getting coffee or shopping for a relative's birthday present. Write a paragraph telling how you would solve this problem.

Requests from Customers

It is important to respond to customer's requests pleasantly and quickly. Notice how the clerk treats the customer in the following example:

> **Customer:** I'd like some help finding a hubcap.
> **Clerk:** Hubcaps are in aisle ten. If you tell me the make, model, and year of the car, I can help you find the right one.

If you don't have the answer, offer to find out. Or direct the customer to someone who does know:

> **Clerk:** I'm not sure if this is what you want. Why don't you ask our manager, Lila Roybal? She's standing over there, by the cash register.

▶ What would you say if a customer interrupted and demanded help while you were busy with another customer?

_____

You might point out that you are busy. Then politely tell the customer that you'll help in a moment.

▼ Practice

Write a response to each of the requests below. Then read your responses to a partner to see if they are effective.

1. A coworker's request: "Would you mind taking this report downstairs to the copy center for me? I'm really swamped." You have time to do it.

2. A coworker's request: "I took your shift a few times last month. Could you trade with me on Friday?" You have other plans for Friday.

3. Your boss's request: "I have a special project I'd like you to work on. What do you say?" You are eager to work on it, but you have your regular tasks to do, too.

4. Your boss's request: "Would you explain the codes on the work schedule to Dora? She's new here." You are willing to help Dora, but you're unsure of a few of the codes yourself.

5. A customer's request: "I'd like two cheeseburger specials to go. I'm in a hurry." The customer has interrupted another customer who was giving you a food order.

6. A customer's request: "Could you give me change for ten dollars? I'm using the laundromat next door." Your store policy is not to make change for laundromat customers.

APPLYING YOUR SKILLS

IN YOUR LIFE

Part A
Think of a request you made recently at home, school, or work. Then answer these questions.

1. To whom did you make the request? _____

2. What did you want the other person to do? _____

3. Why did you make the request? _____

4. What did you say? _____

5. How did the other person respond? _____

6. Do you think you made the request in the best possible way? If not, what could you have done differently? _____

Part B
Think about a request that someone made of you recently at home, work, or school.

1. Who made the request? _____

2. What did the other person want you to do? _____

3. Why do you think he or she made the request? _____

4. Was it a fair request? Why or why not? _____

5. How was the request worded? _____

6. What did you say in your response? _____

7. Do you think your response was effective? If not, how would you have changed it?

_____

WORKING TOGETHER

Break up into groups of four. Two students will act out a situation. The other two students will observe the actors and comment on their behavior.

Actor 1, you work for an office cleaning service. The offices you must clean are extra messy tonight, and you are far behind schedule. You ask a coworker (Actor 2) to mop the floors in one of your offices.

Actor 2, you work for the same cleaning company. You are almost done with your work for the evening. But you don't see why you should do your coworker's floors.

After the activity, the two observers should discuss their comments with the actors. Then the entire group should talk about the different ways of handling the situation.

PROBLEM SOLVER

Are You on the Team or Not?

It was three o'clock and Lin had two more hours left on his shift at the factory. Usually, he enjoyed work. But today he was eager to get home. He had plans to take his wife and daughter out to a fancy Italian restaurant. He had saved for this dinner for a month.

Lin had just finished filling out his time sheet when the manager, Vince, came over.

"Lin, I have a favor to ask," Vince said.

"What is it, Vince?" Lin said.

"I really need you to work overtime tonight. Can you do it?"

"Well . . . I'm supposed to meet my wife and daughter for dinner tonight. It's my wife's birthday."

"Listen, Lin, I don't ask this of you very often, so when I do, you know it's important. And, to tell you the truth, it won't look very good on your review if everyone else works overtime and you won't."

Lin didn't know what to say. So many things ran through his mind. He had been hoping for a raise. If he didn't work overtime, that might ruin his chances. But he had made the plans with his family last week. Vince never said a word about working extra hours until now! Why did he wait until the last minute to ask?

"But Vince, it's just this one time," Lin said.

"Lin, we're a team here. Are you on the team or not?"

▼ For Discussion

1. Do you think Vince was making a request or giving an order? Was Vince's request fair?
2. What would you do if you were Lin? What would you say to Vince? How would you explain your situation to your family?
3. What could you say or do if your employer made many unfair requests?

Lesson 7 Summary

- Be polite and clear with coworkers.
- Treat a boss's request as a polite order.
- Respond to a customer's request as soon as possible.
- Refuse unfair requests politely. If necessary, explain why.

Problem Solving

Barry and Tashima worked together repairing televisions in the back of a TV and appliance store. The back room had only one window that opened. Barry and Tashima were constantly arguing about that one window.

Tashima: It's really stuffy in here, Barry. I have to have the window open, or I'm going to pass out.

Barry: Tashima, you know that I've been sick all week. I sit right next to the window. I want it closed so I don't get sick again.

Tashima: Barry, stop whining. You're probably sick because you don't get enough fresh air! The air in this shop is horrible. I'm opening the window. Just put on a sweater!

Barry: A sweater isn't going to keep my nose from freezing! Besides, you're wasting heat with the window open. (*Darlene, a salesperson from the front of the store, walked into the room.*)

Darlene: I could hear you out front. Are you two arguing about that window again?

Tashima: Yes, we are. Why?

Darlene: I think there's a simple solution to your problem. Close the bottom half of the window and open the top just a little. Tashima, you sit next to the window, and Barry can sit at your table.

After a couple of minutes, Barry and Tashima looked at each other. Then they burst out laughing. They both had been so stubborn about winning the argument that neither of them had tried any alternatives!

They started talking. They found the disagreement wasn't about the window being opened or closed. It was about what each of them *needed*. Tashima needed fresh air. Barry needed to be warm and away from the draft. They thought of some other possible ways to solve their problem. They agreed their coworker's idea was the best. But if that didn't work out, Barry and Tashima had a few backup plans.

Talk About It

- Why didn't Tashima and Barry come up with a solution on their own? Why was their coworker able to come up with a solution?
- Tell about a time when you had a problem with another person, and a third person helped you find a solution.
- Tell about a time when you and another person worked together to solve a problem.

Handling Problems

Think of a time when you disagreed with another person about the best way to solve a problem.

▶ What happened?

_____

Sometimes, you can't help but disagree when trying to solve a problem. You may be surprised to learn that disagreeing can be helpful. It can lead to new ideas on both sides. Here are some tips to think about using when you disagree with someone.

What If You Disagree?

- **Treat each other with respect.**
  Avoid personal attacks: "You don't know what you are talking about." "That's a stupid idea." Instead, tell why you disagree.

- **Find something that you agree about.**
  Even if you disagree on every point, there is something you can agree on—you both feel very strongly about the topic!

- **Ask questions to be sure you understand.**
  Repeat back what you think the other person said: "So you're saying that . . .?" Make sure that you are responding to what she said, not to what you *think* she said.

- **Try to feel comfortable about disagreeing.**
  Some disagreements or problems don't get resolved right away. Be honest about the fact that there is a problem. Then the problem won't stand in the way of work. "Well, Carl, let's just say we disagree on this for now."

Explaining Your Actions

If there are problems at work, your boss may ask you to explain. In the story below, a worker has to explain his actions. (Two volunteers can read the script aloud to the class.)

Joe was straightening the lower shelves in the men's clothing department. Bea, the department manager, was angry at Joe. She came over to talk to him.

> **Bea:** Joe, why did you issue this credit without getting my signature?
>
> **Joe:** There's a problem with a credit I handled?
>
> **Bea:** You're supposed to get my signature on all credits.
>
> **Joe:** I'm sorry, Bea. You were in a meeting. I've waited on that customer several times before, and

she was in a big hurry. But I guess I made a mistake. How would you like me to handle things like this in the future?

Bea: Get my OK from now on. If I'm not here, call one of the other managers.

Joe: Thanks, Bea. This won't happen again.

Bea: You're doing a good job, Joe. I'd hate to see you end up having to pay for a credit mistake.

► What do you think of the way Joe handled this talk with his boss? What tips did you learn from this story?

Joe listened to what Bea had to say. He told Bea what happened. He admitted he made a mistake. Then he asked Bea for advice about what he should do next time. Bea ended up praising Joe!

► Imagine that your boss asks you about a problem. How should you respond?

Don't assume right away that you did something wrong. Maybe you did something right. Rather than assume the worst, give your boss a chance to say more. If the boss is angry, try to stay calm. Answer questions clearly and honestly.

▼ Practice

Part A

1. Do you think the methods in the box on page 58 would work? In which situations?

2. Would using any of these methods cause problems?

Part B

Work in pairs. Suppose your boss told you about each of the following problems. How would you respond? Write what you would say or act out the situation.

Example:
"I'd like to talk to you about how you handled that customer."

1. "This is all wrong. I'm sick and tired of having to do everything myself if I want it done right."

2. "Did you have anything to do with these broken parts?"

3. "I want to talk to you about playing your radio while you work."

4. "There's $20 missing from the cash register."

Win-Win Situations

When trying to solve a problem, one person doesn't have to be completely right and the other person completely wrong. There can be two winners. Is there a solution that will result in both sides being happy? That is called a **"win-win" situation**.

In order to arrive at a "win-win" situation, think about what each person needs. Discuss what the real issue or problem is.

Read the story below and think about what each worker needs.

> Michael and Elizabeth were arguing over the use of the big copy machine. They were both feeling a lot of stress because they had deadlines to meet.
> "I've got to use it now to get this job done by the end of the day," Michael insisted.
> "Well, my work is important, too, and I need to get this 100-page report ready for my boss to hand out at a 9:00 meeting tomorrow," Elizabeth argued back.

▶ What is the conflict or problem?

_____

Michael and Elizabeth both need to find a way to get their jobs done in a limited time frame.

Brainstorming

After discussing what the problem was, Michael and Elizabeth brainstormed possible solutions. **Brainstorming** means thinking up as many ideas as possible. When you brainstorm, you say whatever comes into your head. No idea is too silly or impractical at this point.

▶ What solutions can you think of for Michael and Elizabeth's problem?

_____

_____

Here are a few of Michael and Elizabeth's ideas:

- Find another company copy machine to use.
- Elizabeth arranges to take time off in the afternoon and comes back at night to finish the job.
- One of us comes in early tomorrow to finish up.
- One of us works through lunch hour or takes a later lunch.
- One of us gets the OK to have copying done at a nearby copy center.

When you brainstorm, list every solution anyone says. Sometimes, the best idea will come out of one of the silliest ideas!

Select a Solution

After brainstorming, look at your list of ideas. Which solution best meets everyone's needs?

Then decide how to put the plan into effect. Who will do what? Michael and Elizabeth decided that Michael didn't need to use the large copy machine if a smaller one in another department was available.

Michael and Elizabeth worked together to solve this problem. Instead of competing with each other, they worked as a team.

▼ Practice

Part A

Read the following situation. Then write answers to the questions. Or, the class can break into groups and discuss the questions.

> Luis didn't like the way his department scheduled vacations. He always got last choice because he had worked there the least amount of time—five years. He figured that five years was a long time, even if he hadn't worked there as long as everyone else. He complained loudly to other workers, especially when his boss was in hearing range.

1. How could Luis have handled the situation better?

_____

_____

2. Do you think Luis should have discussed the problem with his boss? Why or why not?

_____

_____

3. Do you think complaining solves a problem? Give reasons to explain your answer.

_____

_____

Part B

Write down a problem that you are having with someone in your personal life or at work. Then brainstorm some solutions. Finally, choose the best solution.

Problem: _____

Possible solutions: _____

_____

_____

_____

_____

APPLYING YOUR SKILLS

IN YOUR LIFE

For each problem, quickly list possible solutions. Remember, no idea is too silly or impractical. Write down whatever comes to mind.

1. Both you and your spouse or friend need to use the car tonight. You have an appointment on one side of town at 7:30 P.M. Your spouse or friend has an appointment at 7:30 on the other side of town.

   _____

   _____

   _____

2. Both you and your spouse have to be at work today. But your child is sick and can't go to school. You each think the other one should stay home with your child.

   _____

   _____

   _____

WORKING TOGETHER

Here are some common work-related problems:

1. Drug and alcohol abuse in the workplace. This is a major cause of accidents and absenteeism.

2. Lack of adequate child care. Parents who do not have child care may be forced to miss work.

3. Paternity leave. Sometimes, both parents stay home after the birth of a child. Both parents should have the right to be with their child, but this creates problems for the employer.

Work in pairs. Choose one of the problems and make it specific to someone you know. Select a solution and then discuss it with others in your class.

PROBLEM SOLVER

Safety First?

Should you stand up for what you believe in at work—even at the risk of losing your job? Jake Snyder faced that problem soon after he started a job at a print shop.

Jake said to his boss, "Henry, I'm concerned about those chemicals we have stored out back. Those containers aren't airtight. And I can smell that stuff when I go back there. I don't think it's safe to be breathing that stuff."

"Jake, that's just your opinion. We've been storing those containers back there for a long time, and no one has gotten sick," Henry said. "The stuff isn't dangerous. It just doesn't smell so good!" Henry laughed.

But Jake didn't laugh. "Henry, the fumes give me a headache. I'll bet the others get headaches, too."

"Look, Jake, no one else has complained. The owners know what they're doing. They wouldn't store it like that if it weren't safe! They could get in a lot of trouble. Besides, they've always looked out for their employees. Drop it."

Jake thanked Henry for his time. But he still had a bad feeling about the whole thing.

Jake couldn't decide what to do. Should he go to the owners? Could he get support from his coworkers? Should he call that government safety agency and ask them to inspect the print shop? He wouldn't have to give his name. Or should he just drop it—like Henry had said?

▼ For Discussion

1. Do you think Jake has enough information to back up his opinion? If not, how could he learn more?
2. What do you think Jake should do?
3. What would you do if you strongly believed there was a problem where you worked? Whom would you talk to? What would you do if your supervisor refused to do anything about the problem?

Lesson 8 Summary

- The first step in solving a problem is to think about what each person needs.
- **Brainstorming** means thinking up many solutions to a problem and selecting the best one.
- When you disagree with another person, treat him or her with respect. Make sure that you understand what the problem is.
- If your boss asks you to explain your actions, stay calm. Answer questions clearly and honestly.

Interviews and Job Reviews

Who Gets the Job?

Gina Marciano, the personnel manager, was discussing job candidates with Betty Rutkowski, the nursing supervisor. Gina had interviewed all the candidates, and then Betty interviewed Gina's top three choices.

"So what did you think of Ron Schecter?" Gina asked.

"I liked him," Betty said.

Gina nodded her head. "So did I. He was here on time. He was very friendly and well groomed, too. I interviewed another one who wore blue jeans," she laughed. "Ron also has experience as a nurse's aide."

"Yes, he was an aide at Dutchings Hospital," Betty said. "He didn't list a reference from there, though. I asked him why he left. He told me it was a 'personality conflict' with his supervisor. He said that they should have been able to work it out. They both kept hoping the problem would go away. When they tried to talk about it, it was just too late. He felt that he would be happier leaving. He was very open and honest about the whole thing."

Interviews are an important part of the hiring process.

"It sounds like you want to hire him," Gina observed.

"Well, he is my top choice. I'd like to give him a chance."

"I'll call him tomorrow and offer him the job," Gina said.

Talk About It

- Based on Gina and Betty's discussion about Ron's job interview, what interview tips could you write?
- Have you had any interviews—for a job, for credit, for a school—or job performance reviews? How did you prepare for them? What kinds of questions were asked?

Job Interviews

You already know that you communicate with much more than your words. This is especially true in a **job interview**. The interviewer's first impression of you is very important. Here are some things you should pay attention to:

Grooming. You should be your cleanest and neatest at an interview. Be sure your hair is neatly combed or brushed. Dress neatly and wear clothes that are slightly more formal than what you would wear on the job.

Time. Be sure to arrive early for an interview to give yourself time to relax. When you leave home, allow extra time. It's possible you may get lost, miss the bus, or have trouble finding a parking spot.

In an interview, good grooming is important.

Interview Tips

During the interview, keep communicating a positive image:

- Address the interviewer by his or her correct name.

- If the interviewer offers to shake hands, shake *firmly*.

- Don't chew gum.

- Don't smoke.

- Look the interviewer in the eye.

- Enjoy the interview. Show that you are interested and enthusiastic. Be alert.

- Be positive! Believe that you are the person for the job.

Questions and Answers

Use your best speaking and listening skills in an interview. Listen closely to the interviewer's questions and give precise answers; avoid rambling on and on. But the interviewer probably does not want one-word or yes-no answers, either. Read the exchange below:

Interviewer: What was your favorite subject in school?

Randall: Math.

This short answer simply states a fact. It would be more helpful to give a reason:

Randall: I really liked math because I was interested in bookkeeping.

Here's another question you may hear: *"Tell me about your goals."*

Since this is a general question, you can give a longer answer. It is an opportunity to really sell yourself. You should take some time before the interview to think about what makes you the right person for the job.

Ask yourself these questions:

- What does the job involve?
- What do *I* do well?
- Which of my personality traits relate to this job?
- Do I have any work experience in this area?
- How does this job relate to what I might do in the future?

During the interview, you will also have a chance to ask questions. Show your interest by asking some questions about the job or the company. Here are some examples:

- What would an average work day be like for me?
- What are the chances for advancement here?

▼ Practice

Find an advertisement in the newspaper for a job that interests you. Think about what the job involves and what you do well. Then write three reasons you could give an interviewer to show that you were the best person for the job.

> ▼ **Communication Tip**
>
> If you don't understand a question, ask the interviewer to explain.

Job Reviews

The **job review** is another form of interview with your boss. Most employers review your job performance every six months or every year. A job review can give you answers to these questions:

- How am I doing?

- What is expected of me in this job?

- How can I improve?

A good supervisor often comments about how you're doing. He or she might praise you for doing a good job but also might make suggestions for improving your work. But some supervisors have a hard time giving compliments or discussing problems on a regular basis. Then the job review might be one of the few times that you and your boss can talk about your job performance.

You should prepare for a job review as you would for an interview. Some employers give their employees a copy of a job review to complete. The worker and the boss then compare notes.

The job review deals with two large concerns:

- **Job performance**—how well you know and do your job

- **Attitude**—how you feel about the job and how well you get along with others

Even if you don't have a review form to complete, you can still prepare for a review. Think about these questions about your work:

- What are my strengths?

- In what areas could I improve?

- How can my supervisor help me to improve?

- What questions do I have concerning the job itself?

Be honest with yourself about your strengths as well as the areas needing improvement. Chances are your boss's praise or criticism won't really be a surprise if you are honest with yourself.

SHOW IT!

Which person will make a better impression during a job interview? Why?

▼ Practice

Part A

Fill out this evaluation form for your job, school, or even your housework.

List your tasks and job duties. Then rate your performance of each task on a scale of 1 to 4:

1 Excellent   3 OK

2 Good   4 Need to improve

Task	Rating
_____	_____
_____	_____
_____	_____
_____	_____

Part B

Write answers to each of the following questions. Add other questions that relate to your work. Think about how you can do better in those areas where you feel you need to improve.

1. Is your work high quality?

2. Is your work free of mistakes?

3. Do you complete all your work on time?

4. Do you avoid wasting time on the job?

5. Do you come to work on time?

6. Can you work by yourself—without much supervision?

7. Can you work well with others?

8. Can you be counted on to get a job done?

9. In what areas have you accomplished the most?

10. What items should you focus on improving in the next six months?

Handling Criticism

In a performance review, your boss may criticize your work. Dealing with **criticism** takes maturity and good communication skills. Listen to what your boss is saying. Be honest with yourself. Does he or she have a valid point? Read the following:

> "Jack, you do good work—when you do work! You're often late in the morning. You take longer breaks than the others do, too. I don't want to lose you, Jack, but you have to start paying more attention to the time."
>
> Jack started to protest. Then he stopped himself. He knew what she said was true. "You're right, Wynetta. I do seem to have a problem with being late. Do you have any ideas?"
>
> "You can start by getting a watch!" she said.

Because Jack knows Wynetta is right, he agrees with her and asks for her help.

▶ What could Jack have said to Wynetta if he disagreed with her?

He might repeat Wynetta's criticism in his own words: "You're saying that you're not happy about my being late." Then, Jack might continue to ask for more details. Or he might simply say how he feels, without making excuses or attacking her: "I don't understand. I felt that I had been improving since my last review."

If you don't agree with your boss, check to see if there are reasons to back up your point of view. For instance, after the performance review, Jack could have checked his time cards. If he had been arriving on time, he could show the time cards to Wynetta.

▼ Practice

Write a possible response in each of these situations.

1. The boss says, "Li, I think you need further training on the computer. I'm not happy with the quality of the work you're turning out." Li thinks he has been doing good work.

2. The boss says, "Anna, I've been hearing some complaints about your ability to get along with the other members of the department." Anna doesn't think there is a problem.

APPLYING YOUR SKILLS

IN YOUR LIFE

Suppose you were on a job interview. How would you answer these questions?

1. What is your greatest strength? _____
_____

2. What is your greatest weakness? How can you overcome it?
_____

3. What courses in school did you like best? _____
Least? _____

4. What jobs have you held? _____
Why did you leave? _____

5. Do you prefer working by yourself or with others? _____
_____

6. Name two people (not family members—preferably teachers or former employers) who would give you a good reference.
_____

WORKING TOGETHER

Break up into groups of three. One person will be an interviewer and another, the job candidate. A third person will observe the interview and comment about each person's listening, questioning, and speaking skills.

The interviewer is the manager of an auto repair shop. He or she is looking for someone who has the skills to take over as the shop manager in a few years. He or she wants to hire someone who would be committed to the job, not someone who is just collecting a paycheck.

The job candidate is applying for a mechanic's job. He or she would start out doing small repairs. The candidate is looking for a position with chances for advancement.

Use the chart below to rate each person's performance as *excellent, good, fair,* or *needs lots of improvement*. Give reasons for your answers.

	Listening Skills	Speaking Skills	Questioning Skills
Interviewer			
Candidate			

You Can't Ask Me That

"Well, looking at your application, I'd say that you have all the qualifications we're looking for," Taylor Abbott said to Carol Dobkin. "But let's see what else we can find out about you. Do you date much?"

Carol was shocked by the question. She really wanted this job at the health club. But she didn't think she should have to answer the question.

She tried to ignore it. "That doesn't really have anything to do with the job, does it, Mr. Abbott?"

He shrugged his shoulders. "Your application says that you live at 114 Catskill Drive. Do you live there by yourself? Or with your parents?"

Carol was becoming very uncomfortable. She knew that he didn't have any right to ask these questions.

"Mr. Abbott, I don't see how these questions relate to this job," Carol said politely but firmly.

"You're right—I'm sorry. It's just that I like to get to know the people who work here. We're like a family. So, you played volleyball and softball in high school. You'd say that you're fairly athletic?"

"Oh yes, I still play softball and basketball."

"Hmmmm. Now, about working Friday nights—what's your social life like on weekends?"

"Mr. Abbott, why are you asking me these questions?"

"Well, I think it's important for this job . . ."

▼ For Discussion

1. How would you have handled the personal questions Mr. Abbott asked Carol?
2. What would you do if an interviewer asked other illegal questions, such as your age or religion?
3. What would you do if you felt you had been denied a job because of your race, religion, sex, or physical problems?

Lesson 9 Summary

- Use your best listening and speaking skills during job interviews and job reviews.
- Be prompt and neatly groomed.
- Answer questions honestly.
- Respond to criticism calmly. Ask the other person to explain the problem.

UNIT TWO

Writing

Writing is an important skill for many jobs.

Imagine that you are a police officer. You might write traffic tickets, jot down the license plate number of a speeding car, or file a report on an arrest. While you spend most of your time at work speaking and listening, writing is an important part of your job.

In this section, you will learn strategies for writing carefully and accurately, in everyday life and at work. Lesson 10 introduces the To Do list—a tool that helps you organize your work and manage your time more efficiently.

This lesson also provides practice in writing labels.

Lesson 11 gives you practice in filling out different kinds of forms. You will learn how to double-check for accuracy and completeness.

In Lesson 12, you will learn to read and fill out charts. Charts have many uses, including scheduling and organizing.

Lesson 13 highlights the importance of writing clear signs and notes. You will learn how to get the reader's attention and convey information simply and quickly.

Labels and Lists

Comedy or Mystery?

Rita is the manager of a small video store. She has arranged the videotapes on the shelves in alphabetical order according to their titles. Often customers come to the store looking for a certain kind of movie, such as a comedy or a mystery. Rita talked to Daryl, her clerk, about organizing the videos differently.

Rita: I've been thinking of a new way to arrange the videos on the shelves. Let's change the shelf labels from letters of the alphabet to types of movies.

Daryl: That's a great idea! What categories did you want to use?

Rita: Comedy, Drama, Adventure, and Mysteries. Did I leave anything out?

Daryl: How about Science Fiction, Horror, and Juvenile?

Rita: That's right, we'll need labels for those types of movies, too. Daryl, do you think you could put in overtime next week? I'd like to get the shelves rearranged as soon as possible.

Daryl: Sure, no problem. By the way, I've got another suggestion. Some customers

How are the videos arranged at this video store?

ask us to recommend videos to rent. Why don't we make a list of the most popular videos and call it "Top Picks"?

Rita: Sounds good. We could put the list by the counter.

Talk About It

- Do you think Rita's decision to change the shelf labels will help her customers? Why or why not?
- How do shelf labels in stores help you when you are shopping? Give examples to explain your answers.
- Have you ever used someone else's list of suggestions? If so, describe the list and how it was useful.

Making Lists

Lists help you to be more organized. Do you ever write lists so that you will remember everything you have to do for the day or week? Do you write grocery lists?

You can use lists to plan more effectively. Lists of things you need to do can help you manage your time. You can decide which tasks are most important to get done; then you can plan the order in which to do them: What *must* be done today? What would you like to get done if you have time?

```
Must do
- clean kitchen drain
- do laundry
- pay bills
- make dinner
```

```
To do if there is time
- mow lawn
- change oil in car
- buy power sander and sandpaper
```

When you make a list, you might see what tasks you can group together. For example, you can save time if you set aside a block of time to make all your phone calls. Or you might group all your errands together so you have to go out only once.

```
Morning phone calls
- Landlord
- Mrs. Taylor about mistake in paycheck
- Mom
```

```
Errands
- post office (buy stamps, mail package)
- grocery store (milk, coffee, peanut butter)
- J-mart (film, pajamas for Randy, socks)
```

As you get things done, you can cross them off the list. This will help you keep track of the activities you have completed.

The next day, review your list. What didn't you get done? Is there now a task that must be done right away? If so, put it at the top of your new list of things to do.

Practice

Answer these questions.

1. What kind of lists have you ever made to plan your day? Did these lists help you get things done?

2. How does making lists help you be more organized?

Checklists

Checklists help remind you about routine tasks or steps of a job. Here's an example from everyday life:

Oscar could never remember how to make recordings on his VCR. He wrote a checklist, or a list of steps, and taped it next to the VCR. He wrote:

```
1. VCR - on
2. Channel on VCR - selected
3. Starting time - set
4. Length of show - set
5. VCR - off
```

The checklist reminds Oscar to go through all of the steps every time he makes a recording.

Did you ever start a project and later find that you didn't have all the supplies you needed? Checklists can help you gather all the tools or materials you need before you start. For example, Neil, who is a carpenter, writes a checklist of the tools he needs before he begins a job. Neil used the checklist below for one of his carpentry jobs:

```
___ Screwdrivers        ___ Assortment of nails
___ Hammer              ___ Saw
___ Wrenches            ___ Power drill
___ Wood putty
```

As Neil gathered each item, he put a check next to it on the list.

▼ Practice

Write a checklist for yourself. Choose one of the topics below:

- a list of things to do or pack before you leave for work or school

- a shopping list

- a list of things you need to take with you on vacation

- a list of steps for completing a simple task

Labels

Labels help you organize your belongings—papers, coupons, files, records, and so on. Labels also help you find things or sort them out quickly. Do you label your suitcases? Do you label boxes when you move to a new house or apartment?

► List things that you label in your home, school, or workplace.

_____

_____

▼ **Communication Tip**

Keep lists and labels brief and easy to read. Be sure you will be able to understand them the next time you look at them.

Most labels are only one or two words. A label helps you identify an item or its owner.

► Often, a label describes a category, or group of things. To write a label, summarize what all the items have in common. For instance, suppose that you had a shelf where you stored paint, paint brushes, rollers, and rags. What would be a good label for the shelf?

_____

Painting Supplies would be a helpful label. It briefly describes all the objects on the shelf.

PAINTING SUPPLIES

At work or at home, you might label shelves so you could easily tell what was stored there—types of forms, tools, supplies, and so on.

Labeling files helps to organize your paperwork. You might keep all the phone bills in a file labeled *Phone*. You might keep a file of car repair bills and warranties in a *Car* file.

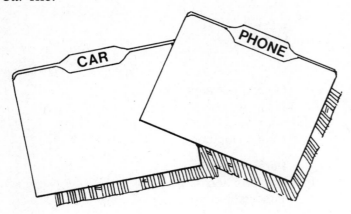

▼ Practice

Write a label to put on each of these shelves. Your label should be brief—no more than four words.

1. A shelf with paper clips, glue, staples, staplers, thumbtacks, envelopes, paper, folders, and binders

   _____

2. A shelf with oil filters, air filters, and gas filters for pick-up trucks

   _____

3. A shelf with window cleaner, floor wax, cleanser, sponges, wiping cloths, and furniture polish

   _____

4. A shelf with prescriptions for drugstore customers whose last names begin with *M, N, O, P,* or *Q*

   _____

Telephone and Address Lists

At work, you may need to keep lists of phone numbers of other companies, repair people, and so on. You could make a list on a sheet of paper. You could put the names in alphabetical order. But it is hard to add names to these lists.

Many companies use card files. The purpose of the card files is to find phone numbers quickly and easily. The cards look like this:

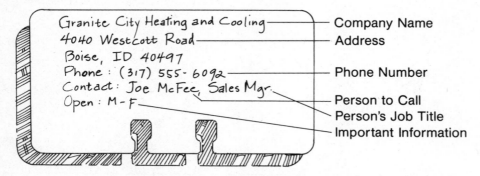

These cards are filed in alphabetical order by the last name of the person or by the name of the company. Typically, you write a company's complete address on this type of card. If you usually talk to a specific person at the company, note that person's name as well. You might also put the person's job title next to the name and add any other important information at the bottom of the card.

▼ Practice

Make a telephone file card with the following information.

A company called Smith Electric is located at 1515 Genesee Street, Chicago, IL 60601. The phone number is (312) 555-8888. The electrician's name is Jack Zieman. The company's emergency number is 555-8887.

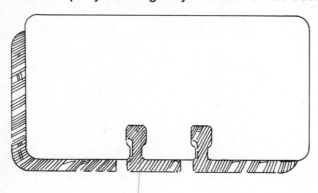

APPLYING YOUR SKILLS

IN YOUR LIFE

Part A

Write down some of the tasks you need to get done tomorrow.

_____

_____

Part B

Now list the tasks in order of urgency or importance. What is most important to get done? What is least important?

1. _____

2. _____

3. _____

4. _____

5. _____

You have just made a list to help you manage your time tomorrow. If you like, try completing each task in the order on the list. As you finish each task, cross it off the list.

Part C

Bring in a copy of the want-ads section from the newspaper. Find jobs in the paper you might be interested in applying for. Then prepare a list of telephone numbers and addresses for yourself. Use the form below to help organize your list.

Job	Company (if listed)	Phone number or address
Example: delivery person	*Luigi's Pizza Parlor*	*555-7777*

WORKING TOGETHER

Choose a partner to work with. Pretend you are both moving out of the same apartment. Write a list to help plan the move. Before you begin, discuss with your partner things you each had to do the last time you moved into a new home.

Where Are the Medical Supplies?

Tanya and Joyce are medical assistants at Forest View Health Clinic. Their main job is taking blood samples from patients. They share a small office.

Tanya is very orderly. She has labeled the bins where she stores medical supplies—needles, bandages, cotton balls, and so on. She has organized all the different medical forms in files. She also keeps a daily checklist with names of patients who need to take blood tests.

In contrast, Joyce is not organized. She often puts the medical supplies in the wrong bin or just leaves them on the counter. Sometimes, Tanya can't find what she's looking for because it's in the wrong bin. Joyce also doesn't take the time to put medical forms in the correct file.

Tanya is angry about the situation because she wastes time searching for things. In turn, Joyce is angry with Tanya for insisting that everything be labeled and organized. Joyce thinks that putting things in order is a waste of her time.

▼ For Discussion

1. Do you think Joyce should be angry at Tanya? Give reasons to explain.
2. Do you think Tanya is too organized? Give reasons to explain your answer.
3. Imagine that you worked with Joyce and felt that she was too disorganized. How would you try to get her to change?

Lesson 10 Summary

- Lists help you organize your time and your belongings.
- Use To Do lists to help you complete the most important tasks.
- Labels and files can help you keep similar things together so you can find them easily.
- Many labels tell prices, addresses, or other important information.
- Telephone lists or cards help you to find phone numbers and addresses quickly.

Filling Out Forms

What Happened?

Officer Chavez got out of her car and walked into Acme Chemical Products to talk to Donna Wisnewski. Donna's wallet was stolen at work, and she had called the police to make a report. Officer Chavez filled out a report form as she talked to Donna.

Officer Chavez: Ms. Wisnewski, I need to ask you some questions. First, please spell your first and last name.

Donna: My name is Donna—D-o-n-n-a, Wisnewski—W-i-s-n-e-w-s-k-i.

Officer Chavez: Tell me exactly what happened.

Donna: I wanted to buy a candy bar in the cafeteria. I took some change out of my wallet. I put my wallet back in my purse. Then I closed my purse and left it on top of my desk. I knew I'd only be gone for a minute.

Officer Chavez: What time of day was it?

Donna: It was about three o'clock in the afternoon.

Officer Chavez: (*writing on the form*) What happened when you returned to your desk?

Donna: When I got back, my purse was still on top of my desk. But it was open, and the wallet was gone.

Officer Chavez: Can you describe the wallet?

Donna: Yes, it's a black wallet. It's rectangular in shape. The zipper on the change section fell off because the wallet is kind of old.

Officer Chavez: Good. Can you remember the exact contents of the wallet?

Donna: I'll try. I think I had about $35 and three credit cards. Also, my driver's license was in there.

Officer Chavez: (*still writing*) Have you called your credit card companies yet?

Donna: Yes, I called them right after I called the police.

Officer Chavez: Thank you for your time, Ms. Wisnewski. I'll file this report, and we'll let you know if we hear anything. In the meantime, please don't leave your purse on top of your desk when you are not there—even if it's just for a minute.

Donna: Thank you, Officer Chavez. I hope to hear from you soon.

Talk About It

- Why is it sometimes important to listen carefully when filling out a form?
- What other people fill out forms as part of their jobs?
- Why do you think forms are helpful for organizing information?

Personal Business Forms

Printed **forms** are used to communicate information in a standard way. On a form, there is a certain place for each piece of information. The person reading the form can easily find the information.

Have you ever filled out an application for a job, credit card, or driver's license? Did you follow these tips for filling out forms?

- Read the instructions and the entire form first.

- In most cases, print everything except your signature.

- Write the information in the correct place.

- Check the form for missing information or mistakes.

▶ What might happen if you didn't follow these tips?

___

One kind of form, a checking deposit slip, is shown below. Nick Fuentes wanted to deposit his paycheck for $670.32, his wife's paycheck for $731.45, and a personal check for $100.00. He recorded each amount in the correct place on the checking deposit slip. Then he gave the form and the checks to the teller.

CHECKING DEPOSIT	DATE _January 4_ 19_9_	4000822 9/90	

CHECKS	
6 70	32
731	45
100	00

FOR DEPOSIT ONLY—NO CASH BACK

_43761-001_
CHECKING ACCOUNT NUMBER

Nick Fuentes
NAME

341 W. Jackson Street
ADDRESS

Detroit, MI
CITY & STATE

SOUTH SHORE BANK

CURRENCY	
COIN	
TOTAL DEPOSIT	1501 77

Member FDIC

▶ Look at the checking deposit slip carefully. Do you think Nick followed the tips for filling out forms?

___

▼ Practice

Fill out the form below. Be sure to print.

CREDIT CARD APPLICATION

Last name   First name   M.I.

Social security number _____

Date of birth _____
        (month)   (day)   (year)

Permanent (home) address

Street _____

City _____ State _____ Zip code _____

Phone ( ) _____
    (area code)

How many years have you lived here? _____

Mailing address (only if different from home address)

Street _____

City _____ State _____ Zip code _____

Phone ( ) _____
    (area code)

Signature _____ Date _____

After you finish filling out the form, check it for accuracy.

☐ Did you print everything except your signature?

☐ Did you fill out the entire form?

☐ Did you check for mistakes?

Forms in the Workplace

At your job, you may learn how to fill out different forms. You may also learn any special words and terms or abbreviations that are printed on the forms. You will probably use these forms to record information.

Some employees record the number of hours they work each week on a time sheet. Study Deena Mayfield's time sheet below.

From: May 2, 199_

To: May 6, 199_

Name: Deena Mayfield

	In	Out	In	Out	Daily Total
Monday	7:30	11:30	12:30	4:30	8
Tuesday	7:30	11:30	12:30	4:30	8
Wednesday	7:30	11:30	12:30	4:30	8
Thursday					
Friday	7:30	11:30	12:30	4:30	8
Saturday	7:30	11:30	12:30	4:30	8
Sunday					
				Weekly Total	40

Employee's Signature _Deena Mayfield_

Supervisor's Signature _Joe Jacobs_

The special terms are *In* and *Out*. *In* is the time Deena started working. *Out* is the time she stopped working—both for lunch and at the end of the work day.

Notice how the time sheet organizes the following information:

- Deena started work at 7:30 A.M. on Monday, Tuesday, Wednesday, Friday, and Saturday.

- She stopped for lunch at 11:30 and started working again at 12:30.

- She left work at 4:30.

- Her daily total each day was 8 hours.

- Her weekly total was 40 hours.

▼ Practice

Complete the time sheet below. First, print your name. Write Monday's date on the *From* line and Saturday's date on the *To* line.

Fill out the time sheet with these work times:

- Monday—8:30 to 11:00; 12:00 to 4:00
- Tuesday—9:00 to 12:00; 1:00 to 5:00
- Wednesday—11:00 to 3:00 (no lunch break)
- Thursday—9:00 to 1:00; 2:00 to 5:00
- Friday—12:00 to 4:30; 5:30 to 9:30
- Saturday—10:00 to 2:00 (no lunch break)

Be sure to fill in the Daily Totals. Add up those hours and fill in the Weekly Total. Then sign the time sheet as the employee. You can make up a name for the supervisor.

From: _____

To: _____

Name: _____

	In	Out	In	Out	Daily Total
Monday					
Tuesday					
Wednesday					
Thursday					
Friday					
Saturday					
Sunday					
				Weekly Total	

Employee's Signature _____

Supervisor's Signature _____

Order Forms

Carla was looking through a catalog for gifts. She decided to order the following items:

Women's Sweatshirt
Soft . . . Comfortable . . .
Warm . . . Colorful . . .
100% Cotton
Small, Medium, Large
Available in orange, red,
navy blue, pink, and
green.
#3765 $16
Page 39

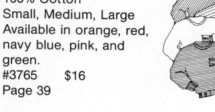

Women's Gloves
A wool blend . . . A wonderful
way to stay warm this winter
One size fits all
Available in green, blue, black,
and purple.
#461P $12
Page 11

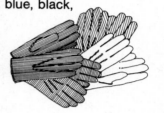

Notice how she **transferred** the correct information onto the order form below.

(708) 555 - 6098
Area Code   Daytime
(312) 555 - 9339
Area Code   Evenings

Name ___ Carla Pulaski ___
Address ___ 4691 W. Addison Street ___
City ___ Chicago ___ Apt.# _3_
State ___ Illinois ___ Zip _60691_

Page	Item #	Qty.	Article (please give color)	Size	Optional Gift Wrap $2.00	Price	Total
39	3765	1	Sweatshirt, navy blue	Large		$ 16.	$ 16.
11	461 P	1	Women's gloves, black	—		$ 12.	$ 12.

▼ Practice

Bring in an order form from a newspaper or catalog. Fill in the order form with articles you might purchase. Then ask another student to check your form for correctness.

APPLYING YOUR SKILLS

IN YOUR LIFE

1. List some of the forms or applications you have filled out.

_____

_____

2. Why is it especially important to fill out a job application correctly and neatly?

3. Have you ever filled out a form incorrectly? If so, explain what happened.

WORKING TOGETHER

Work in pairs. You and your partner will transfer some of the following information onto the purchase order form. You both work for Lubner's Packaging, the company ordering the items. Your company's address is 445 Laughing Rock Road, Syracuse, NY 13210. You are ordering the following office supplies:

- 10 packages of invoice forms, #393687, at $7.28 each

- 2 boxes of white envelopes with windows, #685244, at $11.54 each

- 1 desk calendar, #266414, at $12

Make sure the purchase order form is correct. One partner should read the information aloud while the other finds it on the form.

PURCHASE ORDER

Ship to: _____   Date of order [   ]
              (company name)

_____   Date required [   ]
              (address)

_____
         (city, state, zip code)

Quantity	Part number	Description	Price	Amount

Ordered by: _____   Signature: _____

PROBLEM SOLVER

What Went Wrong?

Min Ja Lee is the new clerical assistant for a lawyer named George Pappas. Sometimes Mr. Pappas has important documents for his clients or witnesses. He gives the documents to Min Ja, and she hires a messenger service to deliver them.

"I want these documents to go to our client Ms. Kadela right away. Here's her address," said Mr. Pappas. He handed her a small sheet of paper.

Min Ja took the address and filled in the messenger service form. Then she called the messenger company. She told them that she wanted the package delivered right away.

▼ For Discussion

1. What was Min Ja's mistake?
2. What might happen because of Min Ja's mistake?
3. Why is it important to check a form for completeness and correctness?
4. What should you do if you are unsure of how to fill in a work form?

MR. SPEEDY MESSENGER SERVICE

Fast Delivery Guaranteed!

SERVICE
- ☐ RUSH
- ☐ REGULAR
- ☒ 4 HOUR
- ☐ NEXT DAY

CHARGE TO _George Pappas_

ADDRESS _____

PICK UP _Min Ja Lee_

ADDRESS _3040 Western Ave._

DELIVER TO _Sophia Kadela_

ADDRESS _2100 S. 85th Str._

INSTRUCTIONS _____

_____

Complete Delivery Received in Good Condition

By X _____

DESCRIPTION	
ENVELOPE	✕
CARTON	
ROLL	
OTHER	

Lesson 11 Summary

- Read the instructions and the entire form before filling it out.
- Check the form after you fill it out to make sure your information is correct.

LESSON 12

Filling Out Charts

What's the Score?

Gloria and her kids found their seats in the bleachers. Their city had a minor league baseball team, and they loved to go to games on warm summer nights. They had arrived late, but Gloria got some information about the game by looking at the scoreboard.

The game didn't remain scoreless very long. No sooner had they sat down than one of their players was walked. Then the next batter got a hit. Two on base. Gloria checked the scoreboard—no outs.

Gloria heard the crack of the bat. The ball was headed their way. Some people ducked. But her son Angel was ready with his baseball glove. He stood up and put his hand high in the air, poised to catch the ball. The ball hit the glove, bounced off to the side, and rolled down the steps. A man sitting a few rows away dived for it and grabbed it. He handed it to his small son. The boy beamed.

Gloria, Angel, and her other two kids were so busy talking about "the one that

These baseball fans watch a game anxiously.

got away" that they missed the rest of the inning.

They paid attention to the rest of the game, though. No more balls came their way. And that ball that got away turned out to be the winning hit. The final score was 3 to 0.

The next day, Gloria read a chart in the paper with details about the game. It told how each team did each inning, and how many runs, hits, and errors were earned in the game.

Inning	1	2	3	4	5	6	7	8	9	Runs	Hits	Errors
Redbirds	0	0	0	0	0	0	0	0	0	0	6	1
Blue Jays	0	3	0	0	0	0	0	0	0	3	8	0

Talk About It

- What charts have you read or filled out?
- Have you ever used a chart to keep score of a game?
- Do you use charts at your job? If so, how do you use them?

Charts

Charts are a type of form. They help organize and communicate information. Charts answer some of these questions:

- **What** needs to be done or has already been done?

- **When** does it need to be done (or was it done)?

- **Who** will do it?

- **Where** is an item stored?

- **How many** items are needed?

Charts are usually arranged in **columns** or boxes. Note what each column stands for. Then read either across or down to find the information you need.

The scoreboard on page 93 is a chart. The numbers across the top stand for innings. By reading across the line that says *Blue Jays*, you can see at a glance *how many* runs that team scored and *when* they scored them (in what inning). Or, by reading down the columns, you can find out how many runs each team scored in a certain inning. Turn back to page 93.

- Find the column for the second inning. How many runs did the Blue Jays score? _____

- Find the column for errors. How many errors did the Redbirds make? _____

Most charts you will deal with are about time—*when*. They help you to schedule or plan.

To fill in a chart, follow these steps:

- Note what each column or row stands for

- Read across or down to find the correct space to fill in the information

Joan set up this schedule for her three children to do the dishes. This chart tells *what* must be done and *when*. It also adds a third factor—*who* must do each job.

	Mon.	Tues.	Wed.	Thurs.	Fri.	Sat.	Sun.
Wash	Pat	Tim	Art	Pat	Tim	Art	Pat
Dry	Art	Pat	Tim	Art	Pat	Tim	Art

▼ Practice

Part A

Fill in this chart so that the four children share duties equally throughout the month. The children are named Chris, Loretta, Lois, and Bob. Each week, one of them is the "supervisor" who makes sure everything gets done.

JOB	WEEK 1	WEEK 2	WEEK 3	WEEK 4
Vacuum and dust				
Clean bathroom				
Mow lawn				
Supervise				

Part B

Charts also show when people are scheduled to work. Fill in the chart below with this information:

- Jack has Monday off but will work 7 to 3 on Wednesday and Friday. He will also work from 8 to 4 on Tuesday and Thursday.

- Dmitri's schedule is Monday and Friday 8 to 4. He also will work Tuesday through Thursday 1 to 5.

- Cara will work 8 to 4 on Monday, Tuesday, and Wednesday; 1 to 9 on Thursday; and 8 to 4 on Friday.

- Stan has Thursday and Friday off and is working extra on Monday through Wednesday—from 7 to 3 and then from 5 to 9.

▼ **Communication Tip**

Print neatly and clearly so that others can read a chart quickly and easily.

Employee's Name	Mon.	Tues.	Wed.	Thurs.	Fri.
Jack					
Dmitri					
Cara					
Stan					

Project Charts

Some charts are like checklists. You mark on them *what* has been done already or even *when* it was done. These charts help you remember each step of a routine task.

Here is a **project chart** that is like a checklist. You can check off what has been done and see at a glance what is left to do. The chart below shows the remodeling stage of each room in a hotel. It shows *what* has been done *where*.

Luxury Hotel—Room Remodeling

Task	Room 1	Room 2	Room 3	Room 4
Plaster 1st coat (brown coat)	X	X	X	X
2nd coat	X	X	X	X
Primer	X	X	X	
Paint 1st coat	X	X	X	
2nd coat	X		X	
Carpeting	X		X	

▼ Practice

Suppose your company has charts for each of the four trucks it owns. The charts show the dates of repairs and tune-ups. You are starting a new chart for Truck 1. It is February 17, 199___. The mileage reading on Truck 1 was 40,119 miles. You have just done the following work:

- Changed the air, fuel, and oil filters

- Changed the spark plugs and the oil

- Inspected the transmission fluid and the brake fluid

Mark each task you performed, using these codes:
I (inspect) or C (changed).

Vehicle _____	Mileage _____ Date _____
Fuel filter	
Air filter	
Spark plugs	
Transmission	
Brake fluid	
Oil	
Oil filter	

Getting the Job Done

For some jobs, employees have to meet deadlines for each stage of the work. A chart, like the one below, shows who completed each stage and when. Notice how the chart shows the remodeling stages of one room in a hotel.

Room 1
Final deadline: Nov. 19
Total time: 8 days (including drying time)

Task	Worker(s)	Date Completed

Plaster
   1st coat
   (brown coat)
	Charlie, Rose	Nov. 11

2nd coat	Charlie	
Primer	Rose	
Paint 1st coat	Bruno	
2nd coat	Bruno	
Carpeting	S&L Carpets	

This chart serves as a checklist for getting the work done. It answers these questions: **What** needs to be done? **Who** will do it? **When** was the task completed?

▼ Practice

On a separate sheet of paper, write a list of tasks you need to complete. You could use tasks you perform every day on the job or errands you need to do. Make a chart with three columns: *Task, Deadline,* and *Date Completed.*

Then, as you finish each task, write in the date.

Calendars

Calendars for long-term planning may also look like charts. A construction company used the chart below to keep track of its work schedule for an entire summer. The jobs the company had booked are listed in the far left-hand column: Cooper Building, Lathrop house, and so on. The numbers at the top stand for the weeks of each month. For example, construction work at the Cooper Building will last from the first week of July to the end of July, so there is an arrow across all 5 weeks of July.

	July					Aug.				Sept.					Oct.			
	1	2	3	4	5	1	2	3	4	1	2	3	4	5	1	2	3	4
Cooper Building					→													
Lathrop house																		
Art Center		→																
Silver house																		
Baptist church																		

▶ When will the company work on the Art Center? _____

Construction at the Art Center will take place *during the second and third weeks of July.*

▼ Practice

Add this information to the chart above:

- Work on the Baptist church's addition will begin in the fourth week in September. It should take about three weeks.

- Work at the Silver house will occur during the second and third weeks of October.

- New construction on the Lathrop house is scheduled for the last two weeks of August.

APPLYING YOUR SKILLS

IN YOUR LIFE

Make a work schedule for the tasks that need to be done weekly in your home. The chart should answer *what* needs to be done and *when* it needs to be done. If you live with other people, be sure to include *who* will do each task. Use one of the chart formats shown in this lesson or make up your own way of scheduling and keeping track of the tasks.

WORKING TOGETHER

Work in pairs. Read the following example of team standings from the newspaper. Discuss these questions:

- What do the abbreviations stand for?

- Is information lined up in columns? Do the columns make the information easy to find and understand?

- Does the chart or listing tell you what happened in the game or what is going on in the division or league?

NBA STANDINGS

EASTERN CONFERENCE

Central Division	W	L	Pct	GB	Streak	Home	Away	Conf
Milwaukee	15	6	.714	—	Won 4	11-0	4-6	12-6
Detroit	14	7	.667	1	Lost 1	8-1	6-6	11-1
Chicago	12	8	.600	2½	Lost 2	5-3	7-5	6-4
Cleveland	10	10	.500	4½	Lost 2	6-3	4-7	8-9
Charlotte	8	11	.421	6	Lost 4	5-3	3-8	7-8
Atlanta	7	11	.389	6½	Won 1	3-6	4-5	2-10
Indiana	8	13	.381	7	Lost 1	8-3	0-10	5-9

Atlantic Division	W	L	Pct	GB	Streak	Home	Away	Conf
Boston	16	4	.800	—	Won 1	9-1	7-3	9-3
Philadelphia	14	6	.700	2	Won 4	10-1	4-5	11-5
New Jersey	8	11	.421	7½	Won 1	6-4	2-7	4-8
New York	8	11	.421	7½	Won 1	4-6	4-5	5-7
Washington	6	14	.300	10	Lost 3	4-3	2-11	4-9
Miami	5	13	.278	10	Lost 4	4-6	1-7	4-9

When Is My Vacation?

Nadine is a cafeteria supervisor at a factory. Each of the food-service employees on her staff gets a two-week vacation every year. In January, they give Nadine notes telling her the dates of their vacations.

Nadine keeps these notes in a file. Each month she checks the file to see who will be on a vacation.

At the beginning of June, Nadine checked her file. She noticed that two of her employees, Jesse and Dana, both scheduled their vacations from June 15 to June 30. This was a problem because she couldn't afford to have two employees gone at the same time.

She talked to Jesse and Dana about the problem.

"Could one of you rearrange your vacation plans?" asked Nadine. "I didn't realize that you both wanted to take the last two weeks in June."

Neither of them could change plans.

"I already reserved plane tickets," Jesse said.

"I'm getting married and going on my honeymoon," replied Dana.

Nadine realized that she was responsible for the problem and didn't want the situation to happen again. "That's okay," she told them. "I'll figure something out."

Nadine decided to transfer the employees' vacation dates onto one chart. That way, she felt she would be able to see everyone's vacation time at a glance.

▼ For Discussion

1. Do you think Nadine has thought of a better way to organize the employees' vacation schedule?
2. How is a chart useful for planning in advance?
3. If you were Nadine, what kind of chart would you make? Draw your chart on a separate sheet of paper.

Lesson 12 Summary

- Charts organize and communicate information.
- Charts answer some of these questions: *who? what? when?* and *where?*
- Charts may show a work schedule or keep track of the progress of a job.

Writing Signs and Notes

What's for Sale?

Randy put the final touches on his FOR SALE sign. He had just bought a used minitruck, so he was selling his old van. The van had some rust and used too much oil. Still, it wasn't in bad shape, and it was a reliable car. Randy had replaced the battery and tires in the past six months.

He took his sign to the copy shop and had 10 copies made. His sign looked like this:

```
FOR SALE
1980 FORD VAN

Runs great! Very little rust!
New battery, new tires
$500 or best offer
```

When he got home, his wife looked at the copies. "They look great, Randy. There's just one thing . . ."

"What's that?" Randy asked.

"You didn't give a phone number!"

"Oh, no!" Randy said, shaking his head. "I'm glad you saw that. I won't sell it very fast without a phone number. Well, I'll just write the number in on each copy." He printed on each one: "Call 555-7777."

Randy chose the best places to put his signs. He posted them at the grocery store, the laundromat, the drugstore, and the community college.

Randy also posted a sign on the employees' bulletin board at work. For that one, he added these words:

or see Randy in the service department

Randy went out for lunch. When he came back, he found a note from a coworker:

```
Randy,
    I'm interested in the van.
Call me at extension 21 when
you get in.
                    Jerry
```

Jerry ended up buying the van for $400.

Talk About It

- Would you change Randy's sign in any other way besides adding the phone number?
- Have you ever sold anything using a sign? If so, what kind of sign did you make? Where did you post it?
- What are some tips for making a good sign?

Signs

Signs are a quick way to give information to many people.

▶ List a few examples of signs you see at home or work.

_____

Signs are often used to warn people about dangerous situations:

CAUTION      **DETOUR AHEAD**

These signs let you know that you should be cautious.

▶ List some warning signs you have seen.

_____

Another type of sign reminds you to do something.

Turn off coffee machine   **Wash hands before returning to work**

You may also see signs that announce events, such as a concert, party, or meeting. These signs tell you _what_ the event is for, _when_ and _where_ it will be held, and _whom_ to call for more information.

▶ What do most signs have in common?

_____

Signs are usually brief and to the point. There is no extra information—only the basic facts. They are easy to read at a glance. A good sign or note should answer some or all of these questions—_who? what? when? where? why? how?_

▼ Practice

Read the sign to the right and then answer the questions.

1. _What_ is the message? _____
2. _Who_ can you contact if you're interested? _____
3. _When_ can you contact him? _____
4. _Where or how_ can you contact him? _____

> **FREE KITTENS TO GOOD HOMES**
>
> 6 weeks old, cute!!!
> 1 gray and white,
> 3 black and white
>
> Call Rick at 555-1874
> weekends and evenings

Read This!

The best sign is one that people stop and read. When you write a sign, you want to get people's attention. Printing is easier to read than handwriting. It also catches the reader's eye more easily. You may want to write in large letters at the top. Or you may use large letters to get attention or to stress main information. You might even use a picture, a decoration, or colored paper.

Make sure that the sign itself is easy to read and understand. Write any details clearly and simply. Then include the information people need in order to follow up if they are interested. Look at the model sign below.

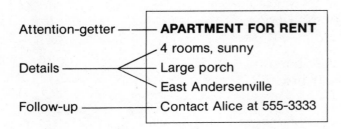

Attention-getter ——— **APARTMENT FOR RENT**

                      4 rooms, sunny

Details ——— Large porch

                      East Andersenville

Follow-up ——— Contact Alice at 555-3333

▼ Practice

Write a sign for each of the situations below. Be creative. Make the sign a suitable size or format for the situation. Be sure to answer the questions *who? what? when? where?* and *why?*

1. It's your turn to clean out the employees' refrigerator. You want everyone to know that you are cleaning the refrigerator right after lunch on Friday. You plan to throw out any food that is not labeled.

2. Your company just got a watchdog that will stay on the premises at night. You are making a sign to warn all the other workers about the dog.

3. There will be a meeting to discuss crime prevention in your neighborhood. The meeting is at 7 P.M. on Thursday, July 25, at the Caldwell Community Center. The address is 1765 W. Hermitage.

Notes

Have you ever written **notes** to yourself, your spouse or roommate, your children, teachers, friends, relatives, even repair people? Notes are short letters. You write them to ask questions, explain problems, and give reminders.

▶ To whom have you written notes recently?

_____

▶ What are some tips for writing notes?

_____

When you write a note, include the information the other person most needs to know. Get to the point quickly. Your note should answer some or all of these questions: *who? what? when? where? why? how?* Here's an example.

Nancy left her car to be fixed. The garage wasn't open yet, so she left a note and the key in the drop-off box.

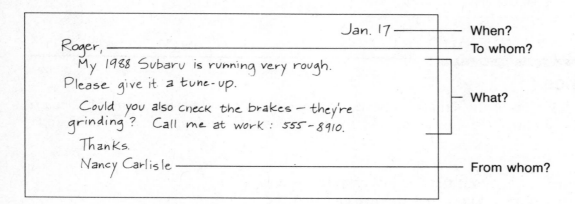

Jan. 17 ——— When?
Roger, ——————— To whom?
   My 1988 Subaru is running very rough.
Please give it a tune-up.

   Could you also check the brakes — they're
grinding? Call me at work : 555-8910. — What?

   Thanks.
   Nancy Carlisle ——————— From whom?

Remember that you probably won't be there when the person reads your note. If the note raises any questions, you won't be around to answer them. Always reread your notes to make sure they are clear and not confusing. Ask yourself, "What questions will the reader have? Does the note address those questions?"

▼ Practice

1. Write a note to your neighbors. Ask them if they own the stray cat that is hanging around on your porch.

2. Write a note to your landlord. Ask him to fix the broken lock and to repair a leaky bathroom faucet.

Notes at Work

You'll write notes at work to communicate quickly with coworkers or your boss.

▶ Can you think of work situations that might require a note?

_____

For example, you may want to give someone a reminder note.

```
Chris—
    We're running out of invoices.
Remember to order more.     Juanita
```

You may also leave notes that give simple instructions.

```
Dave—                            June 9
    Atlas Manufacturing needs rush order on
batteries.  Ship overnight delivery.     Sandra
```

Sometimes, you may have to write a note for a coworker on the next shift to let him or her know what happened on your shift:

```
To: Dora
From: Jan
   I left a list of sold-out items next to the cash register. If
necessary, add to the list tonight.
```

▼ **Communication Tip**

Be sure to leave your note where the other person will see it!

▼ Practice

Pretend you are a machine-tool operator. Write a note to your coworker on the next shift. Let him or her know that the drill press sometimes sticks and is difficult to control.

_____
(date)

_____
(coworker's name)

_____

_____

_____

_____
(your name)

Shortened Sentences

Sometimes, note writers leave out some words. For example, they might leave out *I, a, an,* and *them*:

Replaced light fixture in front office.

(*I* replaced *the* light fixture in *the* front office.)

Plastered hole. Will return tomorrow for another coat.

(*I* plastered *the* hole. *I* will return tomorrow *to put on* another coat.)

Shortened sentences, such as these, contain only the most important words. When you write shortened sentences, be sure your reader knows what you are talking about. Include more details if you think the reader needs more information.

To save time and space on a note or sign, you can shorten words into **abbreviations**. Some abbreviations are common. Others are used only in certain jobs. Find out if there are special abbreviations for your job or workplace.

Many abbreviations are just several letters of the word followed by a period. For example:

refrigerator	refrig.
carburetor	carb.

received	rec'd.
wholesale	whsle.

Be sure that the abbreviation could not be mistaken for another word.

▼ Practice

Part A
Write five or six abbreviations that you might use on your job, at school, or at home. You might list tools and equipment, supplies, job titles or tasks, places, or units of measurement.

Part B
Write notes about the situations described below. Use shortened sentences and abbreviations.

1. Tell your coworker you replaced the distributor cap and changed the oil on the company truck.

2. Tell your boss you restocked the detergent shelves but found that the stockroom was low on Everyday liquid detergent. Remind him to order more.

APPLYING YOUR SKILLS

IN YOUR LIFE

Write a note to a friend or family member to let him or her know what you will be doing tonight and where you can be reached.

_____
_____
_____
_____
_____
_____

WORKING TOGETHER

Work in pairs. Write a note that gives simple directions. Base your directions on a real situation from your job or personal experience.

Read your partner's note. Are the directions clear? Do you need more information? Write a response to your partner's note in which you ask questions about the directions.

Note
_____
_____
_____
_____
_____
_____

Response
_____
_____
_____
_____
_____
_____

What Meeting?

Debra and Will work in the customer service department of a large tool manufacturer. Their desks are side by side.

"Debra," Will said as he leaned back in his chair, "don't forget we have an early-morning meeting tomorrow at 8:30 with the new supervisor. She wants to get to know everyone in the department."

Debra was on the phone with a customer, but she nodded her head at Will to let him know that she had heard him.

The next morning, Debra came to work at her usual time—9:00. As she was taking off her coat, she noticed that the department was empty. "That's strange," she thought. "I'm not usually the first one here."

Debra began to organize her purchase orders from the day before. A small piece of torn paper fell to the floor. It said:

> Debra,
>   Where are you? We're all in that meeting I told you about. It's in the conference room.
>   Will

Debra looked at her watch. It was 9:15. She had forgotten all about the meeting, and she was too embarrassed to go now. At 9:30, her coworkers returned from the meeting.

Will came over to Debra's desk. "Debra, why weren't you at the meeting? Didn't you get my note?"

"Yeah, I got your little note." She held up the torn piece of paper. "But, Will, couldn't you have written one to me yesterday instead?" she demanded angrily. "I missed the whole meeting, and now I'm going to be in trouble!"

▼ For Discussion

1. Why did Debra miss the meeting? What could she have done to remember it?
2. How effective was Will's note? Should he have written one the day before?
3. What is the best way to let a coworker know about a meeting?
4. What is the best way to remember a meeting for yourself?

Lesson 13 Summary

- Notes are short and to the point.
- Notes and signs answer some of these questions: *who? what? when? where? how?*
- Signs and notes leave out whole words or include abbreviations in order to save space.

In this book, you have learned specific strategies for speaking, listening, and writing effectively. Often, you'll use all three of these skills at the same time. For instance, if you're taking instructions over the telephone, you listen to the instructions, write notes, and ask questions about steps you don't understand.

This review gives you a chance to check your ability to perform these skills. You'll see how well you are able to combine all three communication skills.

As you complete the review, try to recall the communication strategies presented in this book. If you want to go over the strategies you have learned, look at the lesson summaries on the following pages:

Lesson 1: The Communication Process, page 8

Lesson 2: Communication Strategies, page 16

Lesson 3: Listening to Instructions, page 24

Lesson 4: Giving Directions, page 32

Lesson 5: Using the Telephone, page 40

Lesson 6: Getting Information, page 48

Lesson 7: Making and Responding to Requests, page 56

Lesson 8: Problem Solving, page 64

Lesson 9: Interviews and Job Reviews, page 72

Lesson 10: Labels and Lists, page 82

What communication skills does a telephone order taker need?

Lesson 11: Filling Out Forms, page 90

Lesson 12: Filling Out Charts, page 98

Lesson 13 Writing Signs and Notes, page 106

After you finish the review, check your answers on pages 116–117.

Communication Skills Review

Directions: Read the following story and answer the questions.

Part A

Diane Foster was making breakfast. Her two children, Anita and Jack, ran into the kitchen.

Anita: Mom, we don't have any school today. I heard it on the radio. They said that Lincoln Elementary School is closed because there is no heat.

Diane: Really? What are we going to do? I have to work today, and it's too late to get a replacement. Maybe Grandma could come over and watch you kids.

Diane called her mother and explained the situation. Her mother said she could be there in an hour.

Diane: Now I have to get ready for work. Why don't you two finish getting dressed and make your beds? Then you can eat breakfast until Grandma gets here.

Diane looked at the bus schedule she kept on the wall.

Diane: Oh no! I just missed my bus. Wait—if I hurry, I can make the next one.

Anita: Are you going to leave before Grandma gets here?

Diane: I might have to. She said she'd be here in an hour. Well, Anita, you and your brother will have to stay alone for a little while until Grandma arrives.

Jack: What if something happens to us?

Diane: I'll put my work phone number on a piece of paper next to the phone. Call me if anything goes wrong. Tell Grandma that my shift ends at four o'clock. Any more questions?

Anita and Jack shook their heads.

1. How did the Fosters learn that school was closed?

2. How could Diane have double-checked to make sure for herself that school was closed?

3. What instructions did Diane give to her children? How did they show that they were listening? Give examples from the story.

4. What did Diane do to check to see that her children understood her instructions?

Part B

Diane decided she ought to call work before leaving the apartment.

Leonard: Hello. May I help you?

Diane: Is this Anderson's Drug Store?

Leonard: Yes it is.

Diane: I'd like to speak with Mr. Anderson, please.

Leonard: OK—one moment.

Mr. Anderson: Good morning. Anderson's Drug Store. May I help you?

Diane: Mr. Anderson?

Mr. Anderson: Yes.

Diane: Hi. This is Diane Foster.

Mr. Anderson: Oh, hello, Diane. What can I do for you?

Diane: I'm calling to tell you that I'm going to be a half-hour late for work today. My kids' school is closed. I had to call my mother to get her to sit for them. And then I missed my bus. Is it all right if I'm a little late?

Mr. Anderson: Sure, I understand. Thank you for calling. Good-bye.

Diane: Bye.

5. How did Leonard answer the phone? How could he have answered the phone better?

6. Did Diane identify herself to her boss?

7. How did Diane let her boss know that she would be late? What reasons did she give?

8. What was her boss's reaction?

9. What could have happened if Diane had not called to let her boss know she would be late?

Please turn to the next page.

Part C

When Diane arrived at work, the store was very busy. She hung her coat in the closet and put on her work apron.

Diane: Mr. Anderson, why is the store so crowded this morning?

Mr. Anderson: I'm trying out a new type of sale. Every Tuesday, I'm going to give the customers double the amount of any coupon they bring in. For example, if a customer brings in a coupon for 20 cents off on a bottle of aspirin, I'll give that customer 40 cents off. I guess a lot of people saw my advertisement in the newspaper.

Diane: The line at the cash register seems longer than usual. Is that a new cashier?

Mr. Anderson: That's Leonard. He's the new salesclerk I hired.

Diane: He must have been the one who answered the phone when I called.

Mr. Anderson: Leonard is working the cash register for the first time, and I'm afraid he's very slow.

Diane: Maybe I can help. (*Diane walks over to the cash register.*) Hi, Leonard. I'm Diane. Do you need some help?

Leonard: Yes. I think I understand how to work the cash register; I'm just a little slow. All these people are waiting, and I'm getting nervous. I don't want to make any mistakes.

Diane: Well, let me ring up these customers that are waiting, because I can do it quickly. Then I'll let you use the register again. All you need is a little practice.

Leonard: Thank you. (*Leonard steps back to let Diane stand next to the register.*)

Leonard watched Diane while she quickly rang up the four customers that were waiting in line.

Diane: Now I'll watch you ring up the sale for the next customer that comes along. If you have any questions, just ask me.

Leonard: I do have one question. What if a customer wants to pay by credit card?

Diane: We have to ask for a photo ID and call the credit card company to get an approval code. It's kind of complicated. I'll explain it to you tomorrow, when the store is less busy.

10. Why is the store crowded? Why is the checkout line so long?

11. When did Mr. Anderson inform Diane about Tuesday's sale? Why would it have been better for him to tell her earlier?

12. What does Diane do when she sees how busy the store is? How does she offer to help?

13. How does Leonard show that he is paying attention?

Please turn to the next page.

Part D

Diane looked at her watch. It was a quarter to four. She was very tired and was glad to be almost done with her shift. She thought about all the things she had to do before she went home.

She wanted to go to the grocery store to buy some hamburger for dinner. She would have to call home first and let her mother know she'd be gone a little longer.

Diane also wanted to get an extra key made for her apartment so she could give it to her mother to use. Diane knew that the hardware store would be open for another two hours, but the grocery store closed at five o'clock. Diane realized that she couldn't go anywhere until she went to the automatic teller machine to get some cash.

14. Make a list of all the errands that Diane has to do before she goes home. Then number the errands in the order that they should be done. Use the form below.

15. Check your list.
- Is it complete?
- Are the errands in the correct order?

TO DO

Answer Key

Lesson 1: The Communication Process

Page 4: Practice
Answers will vary. Examples are shown on page 4.

Page 5: Practice
Answers will vary.

Lesson 2: Communication Strategies

Page 11: Practice
Answers will vary.

Page 14: Practice
Answers will vary.

Page 15: Practice
Answers will vary.

Page 14: Practice
Answers will vary.

Lesson 3: Listening to Instructions

Page 19: Practice
Answers will vary.

Page 20: Practice
The words you should have circled are listed below. The steps are listed afterward.
1. then, before
   Steps
   (1) type up letter
   (2) have boss sign and check it
   (3) make a copy
2. before
   Steps
   (1) have customer fill out and sign slip
   (2) show it to manager
3. then, before
   Steps
   (1) check to see which pens don't write
   (2) remove them
   (3) bring boxes of new pens to front
   (4) refill displays
4. first, then, before
   Steps
   (1) place each contract in its own folder
   (2) label folder by writing client's last name first
   (3) file the contracts

Page 21: Practice
1. It would be hard to follow the instructions. Paul did not explain what to do with the third slice of bread, or which kinds of bread and cheese to use.
2. Answers will vary. Some possible questions:

"What should I put on the top part of the sandwich?"

"Should I use a special type of bread and cheese, or will each customer choose the kind they want?"

Page 22: Practice
Laundromat Steps:
(1) set water temperature
(2) turn machine on
(3) let machine fill with water
(4) add the powdered detergent (put in top basket)
(5) put fabric softener in when rinse light comes on

Lesson 4: Giving Directions

Page 26: Practice
Answers will vary.

Page 27: Practice
Part A
Answers will vary.

Part B
Answers will vary. Below is one way to break down the recipe steps:
(1) slice zucchini and onion
(2) heat 3 tablespoons of oil in skillet
(3) wait until oil is hot
(4) sauté onions and zucchini for 5 to 10 minutes
(5) stir
(6) wait until onions and zucchini are tender
(7) add 2 tablespoons of sesame seeds
(8) add 1 tablespoon of soy sauce
(9) stir
(10) serve

Page 30: Practice
Part A
Answers will vary.

Part B
Answers will vary.

Lesson 5: Using the Telephone

Page 34: Practice
Answers will vary.

Page 35: Practice
Part A
1. Answers will vary. Possible situations include having a major delay on the bus or train and having to arrange child care for sick children.

2. You should call your supervisor and explain why you will be late.

Part B
Answers will vary.

Page 37: Practice
Answers will vary. Possible answers are shown below.
1. Could you spell your last name please?
2. What is your phone number?
3. That's 555-1732.
4. Certainly. When is the best time to reach you?

Page 38: Practice
Answers will vary. A sample form is shown below.

```
                            MESSAGE
FOR  Anthony Lewis        DATE  5/1/9-
FROM  James Pixler        TIME  3:30       A.M.
                                          (P.M.)
PHONE NUMBER  (713) 555-7489
              AREA CODE        NUMBER           EXT.
MESSAGE   Returned your call

                              SIGNED (your name)
```

Lesson 6: Getting Information
Page 43: Practice
Answers will vary.
Page 44: Practice
1. "How may I help you today?" and "Would you like to look at shirts or sweaters? Or maybe a tie?"
2. "What do you think of these?"
3. Answers will vary. One possible answer is that these questions help the salesclerk find out what the customer wants.

Page 45: Practice
1. c
2. a, c

Page 46: Practice
Answers will vary. Possible answers are shown.
1. paper and pen
2. current bill, paper and pen, list of questions
3. catalog, list of desired items with page numbers, credit card
4. newspaper advertisement, paper and pen

Lesson 7: Making and Responding to Requests

Page 50: Practice
1. "Could you please help me with the groceries?"
2. "It's very late and I'm trying to sleep. Do you think you could lower the volume on your stereo?"
3. "I can't finish this job. Could you help me?"
4. "The freezer isn't working. Could we talk about it within the next hour?"
5. "Would you have time to type this letter for me tomorrow?"

Page 51: Practice
Answers will vary. Here are some possible answers:
1. "Will you please help me find a distributor cap for my car?"
2. "Ron, when could you show me how to fill out this form?"
3. "Winston, could you answer the phone for five minutes while I go to the bathroom?"
4. "Please slow down so I can make sure I get your order right."
5. "Are you going to the kitchen? Will you please get me a glass of juice?"

Page 52: Practice
Answers will vary.

Page 53: Practice
Answers will vary.

Page 54: Practice
Answers will vary. Here are some possible answers:
1. "I have time. I'll bring it down for you."
2. "I'm sorry—I can't work on Friday. Is there another day I can trade with you?"
3. "I would like to work on it. Is it OK if I put in some extra hours to get my other work done?"
4. "I would like to help Dora, but I don't know the codes well enough myself. Is there someone else who could explain them to her?"
5. "I'm helping another customer right now. I'll be with you in a minute."
6. "I'm sorry, but I can't give you change. Our store policy is not to make change for laundromat customers."

Lesson 8: Problem Solving
Page 59: Practice
Part A
Answers will vary.

Part B
Answers will vary. Here are some possible answers:
1. "I'm sorry you're not happy with my work. Please don't get angry. Why don't you explain to me how you want the job done?"

2. "No, I didn't. But is there anything I can do to help fix them?"
3. "I thought it would be OK if I played the radio. I guess I should have checked with you first."
4. "I don't know anything about it. Can I help in any way?"

Page 62: Practice
Part A
1. He could have spoken privately with his boss.
2. Answers will vary. One answer is that if Luis has a problem at work, he has the right to discuss it with his boss.
3. Answers will vary.

Part B
Answers will vary.

Lesson 9: Interviews and Job Reviews
Page 67: Practice
Answers will vary.

Page 69: Practice
Answers will vary.

Page 70: Practice
Answers will vary. Here are some possible answers:
1. "I thought my work was OK. But I'm willing to get more training if you really think I need it."
2. "I thought I was getting along fine with the others. I really didn't know there was a problem. What should I do to get along better?"

Lesson 10: Labels and Lists
Page 76: Practice
Answers will vary.

Page 77: Practice
Answers will vary. Here is a possible list:

Things to do before leaving
— take boys to school bus
— bring books for night school
— stop at cash station

Page 79: Practice
Answers will vary. Here are some possible answers:
1. Office Supplies
2. Pick-Up Truck Filters
3. Cleaning Supplies
4. Prescriptions—*M–Q*

Page 80: Practice

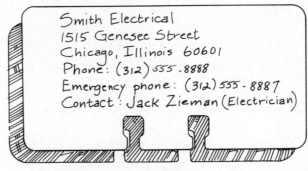

Smith Electrical
1515 Genesee Street
Chicago, Illinois 60601
Phone: (312) 555-8888
Emergency phone: (312) 555-8887
Contact: Jack Zieman (Electrician)

Lesson 11: Filling Out Forms
Page 85: Practice
Answers will vary. Here is a sample form:

CREDIT CARD APPLICATION

Last name: WILLIAMS First name: EARL M.I.: T
Social security number 434-22-1108
Date of birth July 16, 1965 (month) (day) (year)
Permanent (home) address
Street 5251 South Street
City Chicago State IL Zip code 60614
Phone (312) 555-7199 (area code)
How many years have you lived here? 2
Mailing address (only if different from home address)
Street SAME
City _____ State _____ Zip code _____
Phone ( ) _____ (area code)
Signature Earl T. Williams Date Sept. 1, 1992

Page 87: Practice
Answers for name, dates, and signature will vary. The completed time sheet is shown below.

	In	Out	In	Out	Daily Total
Monday	8:30	11:00	12:00	4:00	7½
Tuesday	9:00	12:00	1:00	5:00	7
Wednesday	11:00	3:00			4
Thursday	9:00	1:00	2:00	5:00	8
Friday	12:00	4:30	5:30	9:30	8½
Saturday	10:00	2:00			4
Sunday					
				Weekly Total	41

Page 88: Practice
Answers will vary. See sample on page 88.

Lesson 12: Filling Out Charts
Page 93: Practice
Part A
Answers will vary. See sample on page 92.

Part B

Employee's Name	Mon.	Tues.	Wed.	Thurs.	Fri.
Jack	OFF	8-4	7-3	8-4	7-3
Dmitri	8-4	1-5	1-5	1-5	8-4
Cara	8-4	8-4	8-4	1-9	8-4
Stan	7-3, 6-9	7-3, 5-9	7-3, 5-9	OFF	OFF

Page 94: Practice

Vehicle Truck 1	Mileage _40,119_ Date _Feb. 17_
Fuel filter	C
Air filter	C
Spark plugs	C
Transmission	I
Brake fluid	I
Oil	C
Oil filter	C

Page 95: Practice
Answers will vary.

Page 96: Practice
Answers will vary. Below is a sample chart.

	July					Aug.				Sept.					Oct.			
	1	2	3	4	5	1	2	3	4	1	2	3	4	5	1	2	3	4
Cooper Building																		
Lathrop house							→											
Art Center		→																
Silver house														→				
Baptist church													→					

Lesson 13: Writing Signs and Notes

Page 100: Practice
1. Someone is giving away free kittens.
2. Rick
3. weekends and evenings
4. Call 555-1874.

Page 101: Practice
Answers will vary. Here are some possible answers:

1.

> REFRIGERATOR WILL BE CLEANED !
> Friday, after lunch.
> All food not labeled will be thrown away.

2.

> BEWARE!
> New watchdog will stay on premises to guard at night.

3.

> PROTECT OUR NEIGHBORHOOD !
> Meeting to discuss crime prevention at 7:00 PM, Thurs. July 25, at Caldwell Community Center (1765 W. Hermitage)

Page 102: Practice
Answers will vary. Here are some possible answers:

1.

> Mr. and Mrs. Dunn,
>   I've seen a cat hanging around on my porch. Is it yours?   Brian Stewart

2.

> Mr. Nagy,
>   Please come to my apartment to fix these things :
>   1. My lock is broken.
>   2. My bathroom faucet is leaking.
>   Thank you,
>   Marisol Lara

Page 103: Practice
Answers will vary. Here is possible answer:

> Alicia,   1/17/9_
>   Be careful with the drill press. It sticks sometimes and is hard to control.
>   Safwat

Page 104: Practice
Part A
Answers will vary.

Part B
Answers will vary. Here are some possible answers:

1.

> James,
>   Replaced spark plgs. and dist. cap, and changed oil on the co. truck.
>   Charlie

2.

> Mr. Fancelli,
>   I restocked the deterg. shelves. We're low on Everday liq. deterg. Please order more.
>   Thanks, Tom

COMMUNICATION SKILLS REVIEW

Part A: Page 108

1. Anita heard the announcement of the school closing on the radio.
2. Diane could have tried to listen for the announcement on the radio. Or she could have telephoned the school to make sure it was closed.
3. Diane told her children to finish getting dressed, make their beds, eat breakfast, and wait for their grandmother to arrive. They showed that they were listening to her by asking questions.
4. Diane answered their questions, and she asked them if they had any more questions.

Part B: Page 109

5. He answered the phone "Hello. May I help you?" He could have said something like "Anderson's Drug Store. This is Leonard. May I help you?"
6. Yes. She said "This is Diane Foster."
7. Diane called her boss on the phone before she left home to let him know that she would be late. She explained to him that her children's school was closed and that she had missed her bus.
8. Mr. Anderson said he understood, and he thanked her for calling him first.
9. Diane might have gotten into trouble for being late. Mr. Anderson might have been wondering where she was and what had happened to her.

Part C: Page 110

10. The store is crowded because on Tuesdays, Mr. Anderson gives customers double the amount of any coupon. The line at the cash register is long because there is a new employee working it.
11. Mr. Anderson told Diane about the sale on the day of the sale. If he told her earlier, she may have been better prepared to handle the crowd of customers.
12. Diane asks her boss why the store is crowded and why the line is long. Then she goes over to the cash register and asks Leonard if he needs her help.
13. Leonard watches Diane as she rings up the sales. Then he asks her questions.

Part D: Page 112

14. Answers will vary. Here is an example:
    Things to do before going home:
    buy meat—grocery store
    call home
    get key made for Mom—hardware
        store
    get cash—ATM

    First, Diane has to call home and let them know that she has to run a few errands. Then, Diane has to get cash before she can do any shopping. She must get to the grocery store next because it closes at five o'clock. The hardware store stays open until six o'clock, so she can go there last.

15. Answers will vary.

FEB - - 1993

ADLIT
CON   Contemporary's
              communication skills
              that work.